NIGHTFIGHTER
A Concise History of Nightfighting Since 1914

Below:
This Boulton Paul Defiant Mk IA has been modified by installing AI Mk VI radar and additional fuel tanks in the wings. (Note the replacement panel covering the starboard 28-gal capacity tank aft of the landing lamp.) The increased range proved to be valuable for night patrol work, but the additional weight — plus the drag of radar aerials — further reduced the Defiant's already marginal speed and altitude performance.
Dowty Boulton Paul Ltd

NIGHTFIGHTER

A Concise History of Nightfighting Since 1914

ANTHONY ROBINSON

LONDON

IAN ALLAN LTD

Contents

First published 1988

ISBN 0 7110 1757 3

Published by Ian Allan Ltd, Shepperton, Surrey; and printed by Ian Allan Printing Ltd at their works at Coombelands in Runnymede, England

Acknowledgements

Author's Acknowledgements

The author would like to thank the following persons and institutions for their help during the preparation of this book: Public Relations and Photographic Depts, British Aerospace, Kingston-upon-Thames; Dr Hofmann, Bundesarchiv, Koblenz; PR-Archiv, Dornier GmbH; L. F. Lovell Esq, Research Dept, Fleet Air Arm Museum; Department of Photographs, Imperial War Museum; Geoffrey Norris, Esq, McDonnell Douglas; Keith Midgley, Esq; D. Bateman, Esq, Ministry of Defence, Air Historical Branch; D. J. Martin, Esq, Thorn EMI Electronics Ltd; Capt W. Milewski, Keeper of Archives, the Polish Institute and Sikorski Museum; Danny J. Crawford, Head — Reference Section, History and Museums Division, HQ US Marine Corps; Lt-Col Joseph M. Wagovich, Chief, Magazine and Books Division, US Air Force Office of Public Affairs; Robert F. Dorr; Derek N. James; The Reverend John Rawlings; Mike Keep, for his excellent maps and diagrams reproduced in the book.

Glossary of Rank Abbreviations

ACM	Air Chief Marshal
Air Cdre	Air Commodore
AM	Air Marshal
AVM	Air Vice-Marshal
Capt	Captain
Flg Off	Flying Officer
Flt Cdr	Flight Commander
Flt Lt	Flight Lieutenant
Flt Off	Flight Officer
Flt Sub-Lt	Flight Sub-Lieutenant
2-Lt	Second Lieutenant
Gen-Maj	General-Major
Hpt	Hauptmann
Kptlt	Kapitänleutnant
Lt	Leutnant/Lieutenant
Lt-Col	Lieutenant-Colonel
Maj-Gen	Major-General
MSgt	Master Sergeant
Ob	Oberst
Oblt	Oberleutnant
Plt Off	Pilot Officer
Sgt	Sergeant
Sqn Cdr	Squadron Commander
Sqn Ldr	Squadron Leader
Sub-Lt	Sub-Lieutenant
TSgt	Technical Sergeant
Wg Cdr	Wing Commander
WO	Warrant Officer

Introduction

The history of night-fighting is largely concerned with the application of technology to the problems of target location. As a rule, nightfighter pilots have experienced none of the tactical problems of the dayfighters in bringing their weaponry to bear on a fast-manoeuvring target once contact has been made — although there were the notable exceptions of RAF Bomber Support Mosquitos versus German nightfighters in 1944-45 and American F3D Skynights versus MiG-15s over Korea in 1953. The difficulties have rather been the pitfalls of operations in darkness and bad weather, often with aircraft and equipment inadequate for the task. Under such conditions the hazards of flying often proved more formidable than any defensive action by enemy aircraft. The nightbomber has generally sought to elude the nightfighter, rather than exchange fire with it; and so increasingly-elaborate nightfighter radar and radio aids have been countered by such electronic counter-measures as jamming and spoofing, with the bomber's defensive armament providing nothing more than a last-ditch defence.

Night-fighting began during World War 1 with British attempts to counter German airship raids and later in the war both Britain and Germany were forced to develop fighter defences against the nightbomber. Yet, the early nightfighter combats were hit-or-miss affairs, as none of the scientific aids essential to successful interception were then available. Consequently such defence systems as could be improvised performed at best erratically and were largely dependent on the skill, courage and good fortune of individual nightfighter pilots for their successes. Moreover, the position at the outbreak of World War 2 was little different. Early radar development in Britain had concentrated on the early warning systems so essential to fighter defence in daylight and therefore radar sets for the RAF's nightfighters and their ground control stations only became available in small numbers during the night Blitz of 1940-41. Similar radar-directed nightfighting techniques were belatedly developed by the Luftwaffe in response to RAF Bomber Command's offensive against Germany.

There then followed a complex and deadly game of move and countermove between the night-fighters and their intended victims. It culminated during the closing months of the war in the hard-fought battles between the rival nightfighter forces; with the Luftwaffe attempting to provide a last-ditch defence of the Reich, while RAF nightfighter squadrons hunted them down. Jet nightfighters, first operated by the Luftwaffe in 1945, were rapidly developed during the postwar years and saw limited action over Korea in the early 1950s. However, the most significant postwar innovation in night-fighting came in the early 1960s, when the hitherto separate development streams of day interceptor and specialised night-fighter merged to produce the modern interceptor, which can operate at will by day or night and in virtually all weathers.

As for the future, new developments in night-attack capabilities for both fixed-wing aircraft and helicopters are likely to result in a significant expansion of the night interception mission. The USAF is introducing LATIRN (Low Altitude Navigation and Targeting Infra-red for Night), a pod-mounted avionics system which can be fitted to existing F-15E and F-16C fighters to give them an all-weather attack capability. When LATIRN pods become fully operational — as it is planned that they should by the end of the decade — an important new mission will be added to the USAF's operational repertoire. The Harrier GR 5 — currently undergoing evaluation trials with the RAF before entering squadron service in 1987-88 — will give the RAF a similar capability by virtue of its FLIR (Forward-looking Infra-red) targeting system and pilot's night vision goggles. The US Army's AH-64 Apache anti-tank helicopter also has an all-weather capability, as it is believed the Soviet Mi-28 'Havoc' will have.

Low-flying attack aircraft carrying out close air support and battlefield interdiction missions by night can be countered by modern interceptors, such as the F-15 Eagle and Su-27 'Flanker', which have a 'lookdown/shootdown' capability conferred by their pulse-doppler AI radars. However, attack

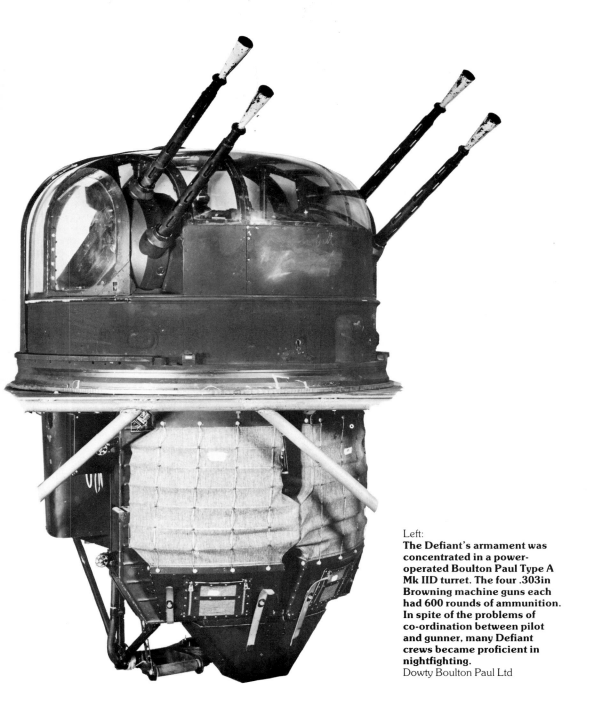

Left:
The Defiant's armament was concentrated in a power-operated Boulton Paul Type A Mk IID turret. The four .303in Browning machine guns each had 600 rounds of ammunition. In spite of the problems of co-ordination between pilot and gunner, many Defiant crews became proficient in nightfighting.
Dowty Boulton Paul Ltd

helicopters may call for more innovative defensive measures. The United States is examining the feasibility of helicopter fighters, based on the LHX project or possibly the V-22 Osprey. The Soviet Union, apparently well ahead, already has the Kamov 'Hokum' helicopter fighter under test. If this does not have an all-weather capability in its initial form, there can be little doubt that it can be easily modified for night interception work. The stage is thus set for an important new extension of the traditional night interception mission.

1 Origins

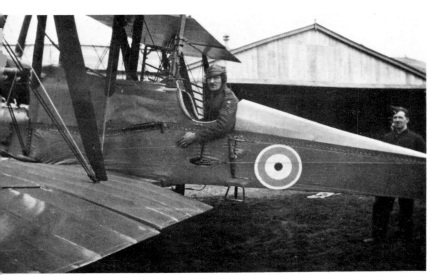

The first nightfighters hunted not the bomber aeroplane but the airship. German airship raids on Britain, for the most part undertaken by the Naval Airship Division, began in January 1915 and continued intermittently until August 1918. It was a threat which the British air services initially were ill-prepared to meet. Virtually all the aeroplanes of the Royal Flying Corps (RFC) had been despatched to France in August 1914 and so responsibility for the air defence of the homeland had, perforce, been transferred to the Admiralty. Yet, the Royal Naval Air Service (RNAS) was poorly equipped to carry out this duty: its entire strength on the outbreak of war was no more than 40 land planes and 31 seaplanes. Most of these were types with only a limited radius of action and none of them was capable of climbing to the airships' normal operating altitude. Moreover, the airships seldom operated over Britain in daylight and few aeroplane pilots had any experience of night-flying at that time. It is therefore hardly surprising that there were no successful night interceptions during the first six months of 1915.

The Admiralty's policy for dealing with airship raids combined offensive and defensive action. It was realised from the outset that the best chance of dealing with the Zeppelins was to attack them on or near their home bases. This was one of the reasons for building up a large RNAS base at Dunkirk on the Channel coast of France, the nucleus of which had been provided by the squadron despatched from Eastchurch to Belgium under Wg Cdr C. R. Samson in August 1914. This unit carried out a number of successful attacks on German airship bases, including raids on Düsseldorf, Cologne and Friedrichshafen. Aeroplanes from Dunkirk also undertook interception patrols at times when the German airships were known to be operating. A second line of defence was established by aeroplanes patrolling between the English coast and London. Lastly, the capital itself was provided with defensive aeroplane patrols — using aeroplanes operating from Hendon — which were to supplement the efforts of anti-aircraft (AA) guns and searchlights. Winston Churchill, the first Lord of the Admiralty, pointed out that: 'it is indispensable that airmen of the Hendon flight should be able to fly by night and their machines must be fitted with the necessary lights and instruments'.

Although the primary responsibility for Britain's

Right:
On the night of 16/17 May 1915 Flt Lt A. W. Bigsworth, flying an Avro 504B of No 1 Squadron RNAS from Dunkirk, attacked Zeppelin LZ39 with four 20lb bombs. The airship regained its base, but was damaged and several of its crew became casualties. Fleet Air Arm Museum (FAA)

air defence was to remain the Admiralty's until early 1916, the RFC was not totally inactive in this role. Its primary handicap during 1914-15 was the chronic shortage of military aeroplanes in Britain, for the British Expeditionary Force (BEF) in France naturally had first call on the Corps' meagre resources. However, the need to form and train squadrons destined for overseas service in Britain did provide one opportunity for the RFC to contribute to the campaign against the Zeppelins. The first such unit to be incorporated into Britain's exiguous air defences was No 1 Squadron RFC. Originally operating airships, the squadron had found itself deprived alike of its equipment and *raison d'être* by the decision to transfer all airship activities to the RNAS in January 1914. At the outbreak of war, the unit had hardly begun to reform as an aeroplane squadron and it was not to be ready for service in France until March 1915. Nonetheless, in October 1914 it was instructed to

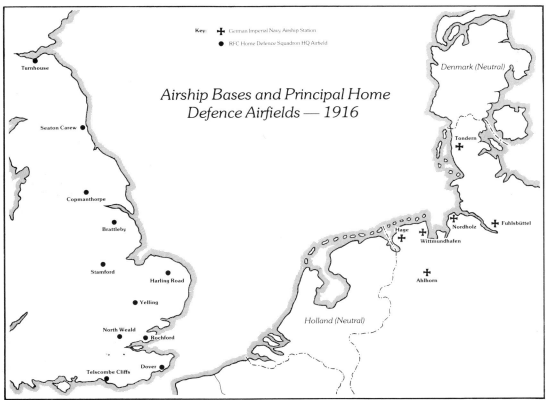

Key: ✚ German Imperial Navy Airship Station
● RFC Home Defence Squadron HQ Airfield

Airship Bases and Principal Home Defence Airfields — 1916

Denmark (Neutral)

Turnhouse

Seaton Carew ●

Tondern ✚

Copmanthorpe ●

Nordholz ✚ ✚ Fuhlsbüttel

Brattleby ●

Hage ✚

Wittmundhafen ✚

Stamford ●

Harling Road ●

Ahlhorn ✚

Yelling ●

Holland (Neutral)

North Weald ●

Rochford ●

Dover ●

Telscombe Cliffs ●

Defensive Effort Against Zeppelin Raids 1915-16

Month	Airship Sorties	Defensive Sorties	German Losses
January 1915	3	2	
April 1915	5	7	
May 1915	5	36	
June 1915	8	17	L37 destroyed by Warneford
August 1915	13	31	L12 brought down by AA fire
September 1915	11	16	
October 1915	5	6	
January 1916	9	22	L19 lost to engine failure
March 1916	13	25	L15 brought down by AA fire
April 1916	25	73	
May 1916	9	14	L20 came down off Norway
July 1916	14	13	
August 1916	20	50	
September 1916	35	57	SL11, L32 and L32 shot down
October 1916	11	15	L31 shot down
November 1916	10	40	L21 and L34 shot down

Below:
A total of five Home Defence squadrons was equipped with the Avro 504K, the type mainly serving in the Northern Air Defence Area. Its performance as an anti-Zeppelin fighter was marginal, but in the event the Avro 504K saw no combat. IWM Q67265

prepare to participate in the night defence of London. The squadron was at this time based at Brooklands under the temporary command of Capt F. V. Holt, an officer destined to play a major role in the air defence of Britain during World War 1. He was ordered to form two small detachments for deployment to Hounslow and Joyce Green. The former was to consist of two BE2 aeroplanes armed with grapnels or bomb boxes, serviced by eight mechanics under an NCO, and was to be in the charge of a flight commander. The Joyce Green detachment, consisting of two Henri Farman biplanes, was a more temporary affair. The aeroplanes were to fly there from Brooklands for a night's operation and then return to base on the following morning. No mechanics were accommodated on the airfield, but each Henri Farman was to carry one as a 'passenger'. They were to be armed with 'rifles, grenades, flaring bullets with Martini carbines and a few hand grenades with rope tails'.

The first airship raid on Britain was carried out on the night of 19/20 January 1915, but it was not until 16/17 May that a defending aeroplane got within striking distance of a Zeppelin. On that night Flt Sub-Lt R. H. Mulock, a Canadian serving with the RNAS at Westgate, encountered Zeppelin LZ38 flying over the South Coast at the unusually low altitude of 2,000ft. Mulock was piloting an Avro 504B armed with incendiary bombs and grenades. However, before he could get into position above the airship to release these weapons, LZ38 rapidly gained height and left the Avro far below. That same night a second Zeppelin, LZ39, was engaged over the French coast by aeroplanes of the RNAS operating from St Pol and Furnes in the vicinity of Dunkirk. A single-seat Nieuport flown by Sqn Cdr Spenser Grey engaged the airship from below with machine gun fire, while Flt Sub-Lt Reginald Warneford's observer, Leading Mechanic G. E. Meddis, engaged it with his rifle. However, no results were seen from this attack and the Zeppelin rapidly gained height and shook off its pursuers. Shortly afterwards LZ39 again came under attack. Flt Cdr A. W. Bigsworth, at the controls of an Avro 504, intercepted the Zeppelin at 10,000ft over Ostend. He was able to position the aeroplane 200ft above the airship and release his warload of four 20lb bombs. These caused some damage and casualties: five of the airship's gasbags were holed and its starboard rear propeller was knocked off; one officer lost his life and five other crewmembers were wounded. Nonetheless, the Zeppelin was able to regain its base at Evère in Belgium. The combats of 16/17 May, while illustrating the essentially hit-or-miss nature of night interception at this time, did hold out some hope for future success to the defenders.

That hope failed to be realised on the night of 31 May/1 June 1915, when Zeppelin LZ38 carried out the first raid on London. Fifteen defending aeroplanes went up, but only one pilot even saw the enemy. Flt Sub-Lt A. W. Robertson, flying a Blériot Parasol monoplane, spotted LZ38 cruising high above him. Soon afterwards his engine failed and he had to make a forced landing on the Essex mudflats. Flt Lt Warren Merriam took up a Déperdussin from Chingford, carrying Sub-Lt J. S. Morrison as his observer. The latter was armed with a rifle and hand grenades, but should these prove ineffective Merriam had instructions to ram the enemy airship. However, the only incident during the Déperdussin's 1½hr-long patrol was the failure of the cockpit lighting. Merriam's goggles then oiled up, still further reducing his chances of making a safe landing. Under the circumstances, he did well to force-land his machine with no more damage than a bent axle. Flt Lt D. M. Barnes, flying a Vickers Gunbus from Hendon, was less fortunate: he crashed to his death in Theobolds Park, Hertfordshire, but his observer Flt Sub-Lt Ben Travers (a trained pilot, later to become well known as a playwright) escaped with injuries.

The first successful night combat was fought on 6/7 June 1915. Both German Army and Navy Zeppelins were active that night, with attacks planned against London. However, the only airship to bomb was the Navy's L9 and it carried out an attack on Hull rather than the English capital. Bad weather was the cause of this diversion, with fog hampering attackers and the defences alike. The Army Zeppelins LZ37, LZ38 and LZ39 turned back before crossing the English coast and only three British-based aeroplanes succeeded in leaving the ground. The East Coast air defences were in any case more dispersed than those covering London, but this weak defensive reaction was also due to fog blanketing the RNAS airfield at Killingholme on the Humber. Intercepted radio messages from the airships had given the Admiralty early warning of the attack and enabled a warning to be passed to the RNAS at Dunkirk. This gave Wg Cdr Arthur Longmore the opportunity to prepare a counter-stroke. He despatched two Henri Farmans to Evère with orders to bomb the Zeppelin sheds and sent up two bomb-armed Morane Saulnier Type L Parasols to patrol the vicinity of Ghent in the hope of intercepting the Army airships on their return flight.

Both parts of this well-conceived operation were to pay handsome dividends. The Henri Farmans accurately bombed Evère and destroyed LZ38 on the ground, it having returned early because of engine trouble. Meanwhile, Flt Sub-Lt Warneford, piloting one of the Moranes, had sighted an airship flying north of Ostend and immediately gave chase. The second Morane had lost contact when climbing up through a layer of mist and, after suffering an instrument lighting failure, came down in a forced-landing. Warneford gradually closed the

distance between his Morane and the airship, which
was LZ37 returning from its abortive bombing
mission. After a 45min pursuit, when in the region
of Bruges, Warneford had reached a height and
position from which he could carry out a bombing
attack on the Zeppelin. As he closed in to attack, the
Morane came under fire from the LZ37's top
gunner and was forced to sheer off; several more
approaches were likewise driven away. Warneford
was by then concerned about his remaining fuel
supply, but as the airship was slow to gain height
and so put itself beyond his reach, he stayed in
contact with it. His last chance came as the
Zeppelin, flying at 10,000ft over Ghent, turned
south towards the base at Gontrude. Warneford
climbed the Morane 1,000ft above it and dived in to
the attack. He released his six 20lb bombs in quick
succession and saw the third of them find its mark. A
terrific explosion rent the airship and it sank blazing
towards the earth. The Morane was caught in the
blast and flung on to its back, but Warneford
managed to regain control. His troubles were not
over, though, as the engine then cut and he had to
force-land well behind German lines. Diagnosing
the trouble as a broken fuel line, he was able to
repair the damage. Then he took-off and regained
the Allied lines before finally exhausting his fuel
supply. His magnificent feat of arms earned
Warneford the award of the Victoria Cross, but only
11 days later this courageous pilot was killed in a
flying accident.

Warneford's VC action was certainly by no
means typical of the experience of the British-based
air defence units. In the course of 20 airship raids
against targets in Britain during 1915, not one
German raider had been shot down — indeed, only
two pilots had succeeded in intercepting airships.
Yet, night sorties had cost the defenders dear, with
15 aeroplanes lost in crashes and three pilots killed.

Clearly the losses incurred were incommensurate
with the results. In the Admiralty's view, the
aeroplane had no worthwhile role in night air
defence, which should be entrusted to AA guns and
searchlights, supported by a network of ground
observers to provide warning of attack. This was
essentially the operational philosophy of the
French, who had built up the air defences of Paris
on this principle. However, by September 1915 the
Admiralty's influence on home defence policy was
on the wane. It had by then been decided that the
prime responsibility for this duty should revert to the
War Office, although the continuing shortage of
Army aeroplanes delayed implementation of the
decision until February 1916. Thereafter, the RNAS
undertook to attempt the interception of enemy
raids approaching the coasts of Britain, but air
defence over land was the task of the RFC. In
practice this demarcation ended the RNAS's
contribution to home defence at night. The official
Admiralty view was in any case that 'not much
importance is attached to flying at night against
Zeppelins'. Accordingly, the RNAS greatly reduced
its night-flying activity during the early months of
1916 and pilots experienced in this role were
posted overseas from the home Royal Naval Air
Stations.

The RFC disagreed with the RNAS view and, by
contrast, saw a great potential in the aeroplane for
night air defence. Moreover, it anticipated that the
defenders would have to deal with night-flying
bomber aeroplanes as well as airships in the near
future. Yet, the immediate problems of developing
an effective nightfighter force were all too apparent.
Night-flying techniques were still in their infancy:
blind-flying instrumentation was non-existent, navigation and landing aids were primitive in the
extreme — and this was only the beginning of the
problem, because aimless night patrolling was of

Above:
A BE12b of the Royal Flying Corps (RFC) fitted with an exhaust flame damper and armed with a forward-firing Lewis gun. The standard anti-Zeppelin bomb was the 20lb Hale. IWM Q68263

little value. The home defence interceptors had to be alerted to the approach of raiding airships, so that they had time to climb to a suitable patrol altitude. A BE2c required about one hour to climb to 12,000ft (where it was virtually in a stalled condition and so barely controllable). So without advanced warning an interception was most unlikely to succeed. The defending aeroplane then had to be directed into the vicinity of the raider and, after the airship had been sighted, it needed the means to bring it down.

Much thought was given to these problems and, within the limitations of the technology of the day, satisfactory solutions were devised. The requirement for early warning was ironically often provided by the poor radio discipline of the attackers and intercepted radio messages often gave the first intelligence of an impending raid. Once an airship had crossed the coast, its position could be reported to the War Office by ground observers. The information was then passed to the home defence airfields. Aeroplanes were sent up to patrol a predetermined line, but because there was no satisfactory means of ground-to-air communications for the greater part of the war, interception remained largely a matter of chance sighting. However, rocket signals from observers and searchlight crews, as well as AA fire, could assist the pilots in locating a raider. If all these measures

worked — and naturally practice fell short of theory — the nightfighter pilot found himself in position to attack a Zeppelin. The weapons he carried at this stage of the war were, however, more imaginative than effective. The basic problem was that the airship's protection against machine gun fire was greatly overestimated. It was thought, quite wrongly, that the airships' gasbags were surrounded by an envelope of inert gas, which would render incendiary bullets ineffective. Hence the reliance on an array of bombs, explosive darts and incendiary grapnels. These devices, while overcoming the imagined problem of protected gasbags, greatly circumscribed the attacking aeroplanes' tactics. For, at a time when the airship greatly outperformed the aeroplane at altitude, a height advantage was essential for the latter if it were to use its armament.

The difficulties and frustrations of the air defence pilot are illustrated by a sortie flown by 2-Lt J. C. Slessor (later Marshal of the RAF Sir John Slessor GCB, DSO, MC) on 13/14 October 1915. It was the last airship raid on Britain during 1915, five Naval

13

Zeppelins being despatched against London. Six defensive sorties were flown by BE2c aeroplanes of the RFC. This two-seater type was to become the standard night interceptor in 1916 (together with its single-seater derivative, the BE12). It had the great advantage for night operations of inherent stability, which made it both easier to fly and safer than many of its contemporaries. Slessor took off from Sutton's Farm at 21.40hrs and began to climb for his assigned patrol altitude of 10,000ft. Long before he reached it, he sighted a Zeppelin above him. He was still over 1,000ft below when the airship 'cocked its nose up at an incredible angle and climbed away from me'. Slessor's BE2c had no chance of outclimbing the airship and he finally saw it disappear into cloud. After abandoning the chase, Slessor had become temporarily lost; however, he soon picked up the River Thames and was able to return to his airfield (later to be the site of RAF Station Hornchurch). He then used up his remaining fuel reserves in patrolling between Tilbury and Chingford before attempting to land. His task was made difficult by ground fog — and the well-meaning but inexpert illumination of a searchlight crew — with the result that the BE2c ended up on its nose! The airfield, Slessor later recalled, was 'a stubble field, from which the stooks of the harvest had only recently been cleared'. Its illumination consisted of petrol tins filled with a mixture of petrol, paraffin and cotton waste, which were arranged in an elongated 'L' shape to mark out the landing run. Accidents were therefore commonplace and Slessor had done well to escape without injury.

During the spring and summer of 1916 the organisation and armament of the nightfighter defences were much improved under the auspices of the RFC. It was envisaged that 10 home defence squadrons would be formed, two of which were to operate in the London area. This was an important departure from the RNAS procedure, since it assigned specialised units to the night air defence role. Initially, the squadrons remained part of the RFC's training organisation, although No 18 Wing was formed under Lt-Col F. V. Holt to control them. The connection with the training squadrons was severed in July 1916 and by the end of the year 11 home defence squadrons were operational. The aeroplanes were to operate on the principle of barrage patrol lines, rather than seeking to provide point defence for likely target areas. This system was intended to extend along the east and southeast coasts of Britain, although continuous coverage was in fact never achieved. It was hoped thereby to intercept raiders both on their way in to their targets and on their withdrawal. Static defence of selected target areas was provided by AA guns.

A significant improvement to aircraft armament was introduced in mid-1916, when explosive bullets became available for use with the Lewis .303in machine gun. These rounds of Brock or

Pomeroy design — later supplemented by an incendiary bullet devised by J. F. Buckingham — could be used to devastating effect against airships. However, the early ammunition was both erratic in performance and somewhat unstable and, so although it quickly superseded the anti-Zeppelin bombs, Ranken darts and Le Prieur rockets were retained somewhat longer as anti-airship armament. The Ranken dart — designed by Engineer Lt Francis Ranken — was an explosive-filled tube weighing about 1lb and fitted with a small stabilising parachute. Carried in boxes of 24, these weapons could be released at heights of between 150 and 200ft above the airship's envelope. The head of the dart was designed to penetrate the airship's skin before detonating, thus rupturing the gas cells and

igniting the escaping hydrogen. It was at once a simple and ingenious weapon, but it suffered from the same tactical limitations as the anti-Zeppelin bomb. The Le Prieur rockets, a French invention, were fitted to the interplane struts of the home defence biplanes and were fired electrically. But, although they had proved effective against observation balloons over the Western Front, none were successfully fired against airships. Hand-in-hand with improvements in weaponry and tactics came better night-flying training and more aids to night-flying. The importance of specialised training was recognised in August 1916, with the transfer of No 11 Reserve Squadron (the main night-flying training unit) to the control of Holt's No 18 Wing. Airfield lighting was also improved and — of equal importance — standardised, while all aeroplanes were fitted with Holt flares beneath the wingtips to give them a source of ground illumination if they had to force-land away from base.

While the RFC was improving its night defences during 1916, airship development in Germany had not stood still. The new 'R' class so-called 'Super Zeppelins' introduced in the spring of that year had

Below:
The twisted wreckage of 'R' class Zeppelin L33 is examined in the field where it fell at Little Wigborough, Essex, on the night of 23/24 September 1916, brought down by 2-Lt A. de B. Brandon of No 39 Squadron.
Bruce Robertson Collection

a greater bomb-load than earlier types. However, since these larger airships' speed and operating ceiling were much the same as their predecessors, the problems for the defenders were little changed. Nonetheless, the home defence squadrons were slow to get into their stride. A series of airship raids in July/August 1916 culminated with a raid on London on 24/25 August by the 'R' class Zeppelin L31 commanded by Kptlt Heinrich Mathy. A total of 63 defensive sorties were flown, but without success. Delays in raid reporting were partially responsible for this poor showing, but confidence in the air defence forces' overall capabilities was badly shaken. Then in the autumn months the situation changed completely: the breakthrough came on the night of 2/3 September, when the German army and navy combined forces to mount the largest airship raid of World War 1. In spite of poor weather, which badly scattered the raiding force, the defenders put up 16 aeroplanes. One of these, flown by Lt W. Leefe Robinson of No 39 Squadron from Sutton's Farm, intercepted and shot down the Schutte-Lanz airship SL11 — it fell in flames at Cuffley in Hertfordshire. Not only was this the first successful interception by a home-based aeroplane — a fact duly recognised by the award of the Victoria Cross to Leefe Robinson — but it was only the second airship to be shot down in air combat.

Leefe Robinson had left the ground at 23.08hrs

with orders to patrol between his airfield and Joyce Green. He climbed to an altitude of 10,000ft and at 01.10hrs spotted an airship illuminated by search-lights to the southeast of Woolwich. However, while positioning his BE2c for an attack, Leefe Robinson lost the airship in cloud and so he returned to his assigned patrol line. Forty minutes later he saw the red glow of a fire to the northeast of London and flew in that direction to investigate. At about 02.05hrs, a 'Zeppelin' was picked up by a searchlight beam and Leefe Robinson, determined that it should not elude him, sacrificed some of his height (he was then flying at 12,100ft in order to increase the BE2c's speed). As he closed in, he could see inaccurate AA fire bursting above and below the airship. From 800ft below, Leefe Robinson raked the airship's envelope from bow to stern with machine gun fire. His aircraft was fitted with a flexibly-mounted, upward-firing Lewis gun ahead of the cockpit, which was loaded with a drum of Brock and Pomeroy ammunition. The opening

Below:
Lt W. Leefe Robinson (second from right) and his BE2c in which he shot down the Schutte-Lanz airship SL11 on 2/3 September 1916. Note the upward-firing Lewis gun forward of the cockpit, and the damaged wing centre section.
Bruce Robertson Collection

attack had no apparent effect and so Leefe Robinson pulled to one side, changed ammunition drums, and fired a second long burst into the side of the airship. This too had no discernible effect. Leefe Robinson then changed his tactics and for his third attack closed the range to about 500ft. Instead of raking the airship's envelope with his third drum of ammunition, he concentrated his aim on one point on the underside. The airship then began to burn and within seconds its entire afterpart was ablaze. Leefe Robinson had to move quickly to prevent his aeroplane from being engulfed by the flaming wreckage. After landing, it was discovered that in the heat of action he had fired into his own machine's wing centre-section, the wire guard intended to prevent this occurrence having become dislodged.

That Leefe Robinson's victory was not an isolated, lucky success was shown on the night of 23/24 September: 11 Navy Zeppelins set out against London and the Midlands — L33, one of the 'R' class, was hit by AA fire over London and then attacked by a BE2c of No 39 Squadron from Hainault. Its pilot, 2-Lt A. de B. Brandon was unable to finish off the crippled Zeppelin. The BE2c's petrol pump had failed, forcing him to resort to continual hand-pumping and after firing off one drum of ammunition, his Lewis gun jammed with a stoppage. Nonetheless, L33 succumbed to the damage from the AA shells and came down at Little Wigborough in Essex. 2-Lt F. Sowrey of No 39 Squadron's 'B' Flight at Sutton's Farm had better fortune that night. Patrolling at 13,000ft between his base and Joyce Green, he saw an airship heading east illuminated by searchlights. He manoeuvred below it and fired three drums of ammunition (mixed Brock, Pomeroy and tracer) into the envelope, raking the length of the airship with each burst. His victim, L32, fell in flames near Billericay, Essex. Both Brandon and Sowrey were awarded the Distinguished Service Order (DSO).

One of the German Naval Airship Division's most outstanding commanders, Kptlt Heinrich Mathy, was to lose his life on 1/2 October 1916 when the Zeppelin L31 fell to the British defences. The successful pilot was 2-Lt W. J. Tempest, flying a BE2c from No 39 Squadron's 'A' Flight airfield at North Weald. At 11.45hrs he was patrolling over southwest London at a height of 14,500ft, when he saw an airship to the northeast coned in a pyramid of searchlight beams. He immediately turned to give chase, flying through an inferno of bursting AA shells as he neared the Zeppelin. He then saw it release its bomb-load and turn away to the north, increasing height rapidly. Initially, Tempest was flying some 3,500ft above the airship, so he was able gradually to overhaul it. At this inopportune moment his BE2c's petrol pump failed and so Tempest had to resort to the hand-pump. This was not only a tiring exercise, but fully occupied one arm and thus made the job of flying and firing extremely difficult. However, Tempest — unlike Brandon — was not to be robbed of his victory by this mishap. As he drew closer to the airship, he found that the AA fire which had been so troublesome five miles behind it was then nowhere near in range. By that time the L31 had almost reached his altitude of 15,000ft and was continuing to climb rapidly. Tempest therefore dived straight into the attack, giving the petrol pump an especially vigorous action, before abandoning it and opening fire with his machine gun. He positioned his aeroplane under the Zeppelin's tail, seeing the tracers from the airship gunners' erratic return fire flying all around. He then saw the L31 begin to burn. 'The airship', Tempest reported, 'shot up about 200ft, paused, and came roaring down straight on to me before I had time to get out of the way. I nose-dived for all I was worth . . . put my machine in a spin and just managed to corkscrew

17

Defensive Effort Against Zeppelin Raids 1917-18			
Month	Airship Sorties	Defensive Sorties	German Losses
February 1917	1	6	
March 1917	5	17	L39 shot down by AA over France
May 1917	6	76	
June 1917	4	32	L48 shot down
August 1917	8	21	
September 1917	11	36	
October 1917	11	78	5 airships lost in high winds
March 1918	8	24	
April 1918	5	27	
August 1918	5	35	L70 shot down

out of the way as she shot past me, roaring like a furnace.'

Two more Zeppelins were lost on the night of 27/28 November, one falling to the guns of 2-Lt V. I. Pyott of No 36 Squadron off Hartlepool. So as 1916 ended it seemed that the defenders had finally taken the measure of the Zeppelin. Improved airships capable of operating at altitudes of up to 20,000ft were introduced in 1917, but they proved to be generally ineffective. High winds, poor weather and navigational difficulties proved to be more deadly enemies to these 'high climber'

Zeppelins than the British air defences. Of the seven German airships lost in 1917, only one was shot down by an aeroplane — this falling to Lt L. P. Watkins of No 37 Squadron on 16/17 June. From

Below:
The Sopwith Camel flown by Capt G. S. M. Insall VC of No 50 Squadron from Bekesbourne. It shows the principal features of Camels modified for the night-fighting role, including the cutaway wing centre section, twin Lewis gun armament and cockpit moved rearwards by 1ft 6in. IWM Q57659

Left:
Gilbert Insall, who won his VC In France in 1915, became a flight commander with No 50 Squadron in 1918. IWM Q66142

the spring of 1917 the main bombing threat came from Gotha twin-engined bombers operating by daylight. The well-tried BE2c and BE12 aeroplanes of the home defence squadrons were of little use in countering this new offensive. However, the diversion from the Western Front of up-to-date single-seat fighters, such as Sopwith's Pup and Camel and the Royal Aircraft Factory's SE5, together with a thoroughgoing reorganisation of the capital's defences into Maj-Gen E. B. Ashmore's London Air Defence Area, combined to bring about the defeat of the daylight raiders by the end of August. The Gothas then predictably switched their attacks to the hours of darkness. The move was well calculated to render the RFC's carefully nurtured home defence forces obsolete, for few of the specialised night-fighting aircraft had the necessary performance to match the Gothas. Only 12 FE2ds, out of a total force of some 190 aeroplanes, fell into this category. And in any case the elusive bomber aircraft would be far less conspicuous night targets than the massive and relatively ponderous Zeppelins.

The defenders' record on the night of 3/4 September, when five Gothas made their first

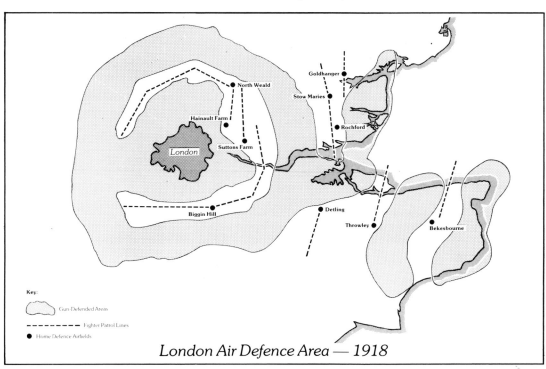

Key:
⌒ Gun-Defended Areas
------- Fighter Patrol Lines
● Home Defence Airfields

London Air Defence Area — 1918

Night Aeroplane Raids on Britain and Defensive Effort 1917-18			
Month	Sorties Despatched	Defensive Sorties	German Casualties
September 1917	95	177	7 Gothas lost 7 Gothas crashed on return
October 1917	43	76	5 Gothas crashed on return
December 1917	39	99	5 Gothas lost 8 Gothas crashed on return
January 1918	19	183	1 Gotha lost 5 Gothas crashed on return
February 1918	6	129	None
March 1918	6	42	2 Gothas crashed on return
May 1918	14	88	4 Gothas lost 1 Gotha crashed on return

Note: Five of the Gothas lost were shot down by nightfighters; 11 British nightfighters crashed during defensive patrols

nocturnal raid on Britain, seemed to bear out the most gloomy prognostications. Yet, thanks to the personal initiative and courage of Capt Gilbert Murlis Green, the Acting Commanding Officer of No 44 Squadron, the RFC's dilemma was to be resolved. No 44 Squadron was a dayfighter unit, which had been formed in July 1917 for home defence duties and equipped with Sopwith Camels. No one in authority believed that the high-performance Camel, which was notoriously tricky to fly, could successfully operate at night. Yet Murlis Green and two of his pilots, Capt C. J. Q. Brand and 2-Lt C. C. Banks, proved that it was possible. Brand, who as AVM Quintin Brand was to command No 10 Group Fighter Command in the Battle of Britain, recalled 'we patrolled for about forty minutes and then returned for news and incidentally to find out if we could effect a safe landing. This successfully accomplished convinced us of the delightful qualities of our machine'. Nevertheless, much remained to be done before an efficient nightfighter force could be assembled to meet the German bombers. The so-called 'Harvest Moon' raids of September and October 1917 were virtually unopposed for, although the home defence squadrons flew more than 150 sorties, not one German bomber was brought down by them. The first nightfighter success came on 18/19 December and, fittingly, the successful pilot was Murlis Green.

Ashmore, the commander of London's air defences, saw clearly that the nightfighter offered the best means of defence against the Gothas and the massive R-planes or Giants which had begun operations against Britain in September 1917. However, these needed to be high-performance aeroplanes and it was decided to standardise on the Camel, SE5a and Bristol F2B Fighter. As the RFC squadrons in France had an equally pressing need for such aeroplanes, re-equipment of the home defence squadrons was slow. In January 1918 Ashmore stated that he had only 63 modern nightfighters for the defence of London. Improvements to searchlights and the ground observer system were also implemented, which increased the chances of detecting the elusive night-bombers. Ashmore wisely decided to separate the AA gun zones from the nightfighter patrol areas. Accordingly the guns were concentrated in outer and inner barrage zones, leaving clear lanes between them, in which the aeroplanes patrolled. Modifications to the standard dayfighters were necessary before they could be used for night-fighting. For example, the Camel's weight was brought down by reducing its petrol tankage, the fuselage-mounted twin Vickers guns were replaced by Lewis guns carried on the top wing and the wing centre-section was cut away to improve the upward view. An improved night-sight, designed by Lt H. B. Neame, was introduced. It consisted of an illuminating ring, which would be exactly filled by the Gotha's 77ft wingspan at 100yd range. It was a better device than the earlier Hutton bead and 'V' backsight arrangement, although some problems were encountered when the very much larger R-planes were the target.

The acid test for the improved night defences came on 19/20 May, when 38 Gothas and three Giants carried out the largest nightbomber raid of the war. The home defence squadrons flew 88 sorties and succeeded in bringing down three Gothas. Brand, by that time a major and Commanding Officer of No 112 Squadron, gained one of the victories. His Camel took off from

RAF Home Defence Squadrons November 1918

Squadron		Aircraft	Base
No 33	Squadron	Avro 504K	Scampton; Kirton in Lindsey; Elsham
No 36	Squadron	Bristol Fighter; Sopwith Pup	Usworth; Ashington; Seaton Carew
No 37	Squadron	Sopwith Camel	Stow Maries; Goldhanger
No 44	Squadron	Sopwith Camel	Hainault Farm
No 50	Squadron	Sopwith Camel	Bekesbourne
No 51	Squadron	FE2b; Sopwith Camel	Mattishall; Tydd St Mary; Marham
No 61	Squadron	Sopwith Camel	Rochford
No 75	Squadron	Avro 504K	Hadleigh; Elmswell
No 76	Squadron	Avro 504K	Copmanthorpe; Helperby; Catterick
No 77	Squadron	Avro 504K	Whiteburn; Penston
No 78	Squadron	Sopwith Camel	Suttons Farm
No 90	Squadron	Avro 504K	Leadenham; Buckminster; Wittering
No 112	Squadron	Sopwith Camel	Throwley
No 141	Squadron	Bristol Fighter	Biggin Hill
No 143	Squadron	Sopwith Camel	Detling

Below:
Introduced during the interwar years, the Chance Light was a searchlight intended for ground illumination during night-flying. The actual landing path was marked by flares. Ministry of Defence (MoD)

Above:
Maj B. E. Baker, the CO of No 141 Squadron which flew Bristol F2B Fighters from Biggin Hill, holds aloft the unit's fighting cock mascot. No 141 Squadron became the 'Cock Squadron' after winning the No 6 Brigade efficiency competition in September 1918. IWM Q27430

Throwley at 23.15hrs and he climbed to patrol height of about 8,000ft. He then saw a concentration of four searchlight beams to the northeast and shortly afterwards picked out a twin-engined bomber flying 500ft above him. Brand turned in behind it, approaching from below and astern. The German rear gunner then opened fire from the ventral gun position. Brand, returning his fire, saw the Gotha catch fire and its starboard engine fail. The German bomber then rapidly turned and dived towards the ground. Brand's Camel was so close to it that his machine was momentarily enveloped in the flames and his face and moustache were singed. After watching his victim crash, Brand regained height and continued his patrol. He was awarded the DSO for this action. Two Bristol Fighter crews were also successful that night: Lt A. J. Arkell and his gunner Air Mechanic A. T. G. Stagg of No 39 Squadron sent a Gotha down to crash at East Ham, and Lt E. E. Turner and Lt H. B. Barwise of No 141 Squadron, Biggin Hill, accounted for another. The latter claim was disputed by Maj F. Sowrey of No 143 Squadron, whose SE5a had earlier attacked this Gotha.

The 19/20 May raid proved to be the last raid by German bombers on Britain. However, this change of policy was due not to the improved nightfighter defences, but to the pressing needs of the armies in France. Henceforth, the German bombers concen-

trated their efforts on attacking the rear areas of the Allied armies on the Western Front. In order to meet this new threat, experienced pilots were withdrawn from three home defence squadrons in order to form No 151 Squadron. The unit, equipped with Camel nightfighters moved to France in June 1918 under the command of Murlis Green. By the time of the Armistice they had gained 26 victories, although their efforts did not stop the depredations of the German bombers. The squadron's first successful combat was fought on 23 July, Capt A. B. Yuill shooting down a German bomber near Étaples. The same pilot also succeeded in bringing down a Giant on 10 August. Searchlight illumination had attracted four pilots to the vicinity of the bomber, but Yuill made sure of his victory by closing in to close range below and behind the Giant before opening fire. He fired three short bursts aimed at the engines and a further two into the fuselage. The enemy bomber went into a steep dive, began to burn and, as Yuill followed it down he saw a wing break away. As well as mounting defensive night patrols, the Squadron carried out offensive sweeps over the German bomber airfields and flew in support of the RAF night-bombers of No 101 Squadron, thereby pioneering two of the night-fighter's significant operational roles of World War 2. Following No 151 Squadron's successes, it was decided to increase the strength of the nightfighters in France to five squadrons. A second unit, No 152 Squadron, arrived in October 1918, but the Armistice prevented any further expansion.

The diversion of the German bombers to targets in France did not remove the need for strong night air defences in Britain, as there could be no guarantee that attacks would not be resumed. Consequently, the home defence forces continued to be built up and at the time of the Armistice there were 15 squadrons, 10 of which were assigned to the London Air Defence Area (LADA) with the remainder supporting the Northern Air Defence Area. Improvements in equipment and tactics also continued apace, the most significant innovation of the period being the introduction of wireless telephony (later known as radio telephony). No 141 Squadron's Bristol Fighters were the first to be so equipped and by August 1918 all the LADA squadrons had this equipment. It was a tremendous breakthrough in nightfighter tactics, as for the first time the ground commander of the air defences could pass information and orders to aeroplanes in the air. However, information on the position of enemy aircraft still depended on the ground observer network and this weakness was not to be overcome until the introduction of specialised radars in World War 2.

The years between the two world wars were generally a period of stagnation, so far as night-fighting techniques and tactics were concerned. The drastic rundown of the RAF after the Armistice and a chronic shortage of funding throughout most of the 1920s and 1930s meant that few resources could be devoted to such a specialised role. Night-fighting during this period was the responsibility of the dayfighter squadrons. It was an unsatisfactory situation, as AM Sir Geoffrey Salmond recognised when assessing the results of the 1932 air exercises. He wrote: 'Fighter squadrons could not fight by day and by night. Entirely separate squadrons were required for each function.' It was the opinion of one pilot that at this

Below:
In October 1918 No 37 Squadron re-equipped with Camels in preparation for a possible upsurge in enemy bomber activity. Here, squadron pilots are seen with their machines. Note the shading out of the white in the rudder flash of the foremost aircraft. Crown Copyright via Bruce Robertson

period the specialised lessons of night-fighting so painfully gained during World War 1 had been largely forgotten. Certainly, the contemporary RAF Flying Training Manual does no more than recapitulate the more obvious lessons to be drawn from that conflict. There was, however, one important development in the interwar period, which was to affect the future of night-fighting. This was the introduction of blind-flying training by the Central Flying School (CFS) in 1930. From then on,

at least some of the hazards of night-flying — which had often proved to be more formidable than the danger of enemy action — had been removed.

Below:
Shortly after the Armistice No 37 Squadron's Sopwith Camels were replaced with Snipes; one of these night-fighters is pictured at Biggin Hill in 1919. Note the Holt flares fitted beneath the wings. MoD

A Hawker Woodcock of No 17 Squadron RAF, which operated this type at Upavon from March 1926 until January 1928. The unit carried out both day and nightfighter work. BAe

The Sopwith Dolphin was well suited to the nightfighter role, in the view of Brig-Gen T. C. R. Higgins, commanding No 6 Brigade. However, the aircraft's tricky handling characteristics led to its rejection for this work on the recommendation of Maj Philip Babington, CO of No 141 Squadron. British Aerospace (BAe)

Above:
No 17 Squadron (illustrated) and No 3 Squadron were the only RAF units to operate the Woodcock II, which was the first RAF fighter to be designed from the outset for night operation. BAe

Below:
The Bristol Bulldog IIA, which entered RAF service in 1929, was intended from the outset for both day and night operation. This photograph of the prototype J9480, clearly shows the underwing flare brackets and the navigation lights fitted to the upper wing and rudder. BAe

2 Nightfighters in the Blitz

At the outbreak of World War 2 the RAF's night defences depended upon the dayfighter squadrons, operating on 'Cat's Eyes' patrols in darkness and working in co-operation with the searchlights. In at least one important respect it was a less satisfactory system than that of 1918, since there were no longer any specialised nightfighter units. Moreover, this shortcoming was only partially made good in the early months of the war by assigning to night defence duties those units of Fighter Command which were manifestly ill-equipped for dayfighter operations. Initially comprising six squadrons of Bristol Blenheim Mk 1f twin-engined fighters, the

Below:
The mainstay of the RAF's nightfighter force during the early period of World War 2 was the Blenheim If, a converted twin-engined bomber. Its main armament comprised four .303in machine guns carried in a ventral pack mounted beneath the bomb bay. Illustrated Blenheim If of No 54

Operational Training Unit (OTU), the first specialised nightfighter OTU, which was formed at Church Fenton early in 1941, later moving to Charterhall. Its aircraft were 'hand-me-downs' from the frontline units which had re-equipped with Beaufighters. MoD

At the time of their inception, the RAF's Hurricane and Spitfire single-seat fighters were intended for both day and night operation. The Hurricane in particular, with its robust undercarriage, was found to be a fairly efficient nightfighter and many operated in this role. The illustration of a Canadian-built Hurricane XII of the RCAF clearly shows the shields fitted forward of the cockpit to reduce glare from the engine exhausts. BAe

RAF's specialised nightfighter force was augmented by two squadrons of Boulton Paul Defiant turret fighters in the summer of 1940, when they too had proved unsuitable as dayfighters. That neither type was a particularly effective nightfighter is unsurprising, since they had not been designed for that purpose. The Blenheim, indeed, was nothing more than a stopgap fighter, having been drawn from surplus bomber stocks to provide interim equipment for Fighter Command during the RAF's prewar expansion phase. But, if the RAF was badly equipped for night defence, it was certainly in no way inferior to any other air force of the period in that respect. And, unlike the air arms of the other warring powers, the RAF had at least given careful thought to the problem of dealing with the night-bomber. Important scientific and technological developments were in hand, which were to revolutionise the business of night-fighting. However, the paramount needs of the daylight air defences and the extreme technical complexity of the new systems, meant that for the first year of war the nightfighters would be quite literally groping in the dark.

The impending breakthrough in night-fighting techniques was of course dependent on the newly-devised radar (then known by the cover name Radio Direction Finding, or RDF). As early as February 1936, Robert Watson-Watt put forward the idea of an airborne radar to the Tizard Committee for the Scientific Survey of Air Defence. The difficulties of adapting a system — which in its initial early-warning version weighed several hundred tons — for installation in an aeroplane were obviously tremendous, even though the airborne

set need only have one-twentieth of the range. And the problems of Dr D. G. Bowen, who was put in charge of this development project, were compounded by the overriding priority in resources accorded to the Chain Home early-warning radar. Nevertheless, by August 1937 an airborne radar set was ready for trials, albeit one capable of detecting ships rather than aircraft. The more complex requirements of an Airborne Interception (AI) radar were not met until May 1939, when the first experimental set was installed in a Fairey Battle light bomber. During trials it proved capable of detecting a Handley Page Harrow at ranges of between three miles and 900ft and it also indicated the relative position of the target in elevation and azimuth. ACM Sir Hugh Dowding, AOC-in-C Fighter Command, was impressed with the new equipment and envisaged its use by twin-engined fighters manned by a team of pilot and radar operator. Yet despite the remarkable progress made with the development of AI radar, it was still a long way from full-scale operational service.

Operational trials with the first hand-made AI Mk I radars began in September 1939. Three Blenheim

IVs fitted with this equipment were assigned to No 25 Squadron at Northolt. In November 1939 the AI-equipped Blenheims were detached to Martlesham Heath for night patrols over the North Sea, but they made no contact with enemy aircraft. Their targets were the minelaying seaplanes, which had begun to operate over the Thames Estuary and East Coast at this time. However, an inherent limitation of the AI radar was its poor performance at low altitude, where ground returns swamped any echo from the target aircraft. And, since the minelayers invariably operated at low altitude, the AI Blenheims had little chance of success. In any case the AI Mk I was extremely temperamental and, even under better operating conditions, was liable to perform erratically or fail completely. The AI-equipped Blenheims persevered, operating with No 600 Squadron from Manston over the Thames Estuary and the Bawdsey Radar Flight from Martlesham Heath, as well as with No 25 Squadron. The AI development team had been evacuated from Bawdsey on the outbreak of war, as the experimental radar station's exposed situation on

the Suffolk coast rendered it vulnerable to air attack or commando-style raids. Its first move was to Perth, but the damp of a Scottish winter played havoc with its delicate electronic equipment and so a new home was found at St Athan in Wales in November 1939. From there AI-equipped Blenheims were detached to Martlesham Heath for operational patrols. It was not until the spring of 1940, however, that they saw combat. On 12 May one of the Flight's Blenheim IVs, flown by Flt Lt C. D. S. Smith DFC, intercepted a Heinkel He111 off the Dutch coast. Smith attacked and the enemy aircraft was last seen trailing black smoke and losing height. Return fire from the German bomber wounded Smith and his Blenheim crashed on return to base. As the fate of the German bomber is uncertain, this combat cannot be claimed as the first success by a radar-equipped nightfighter. In any case, the official account of the action, while stating that the Blenheim was operating under the control of the Bawdsey Chain Home Station, makes no mention of AI being used during the interception.

Left:
The cockpit interior of a Blenheim I. Note the standard blind-flying panel mounted centrally in front of the pilot. It was found that reflections from the extensively-glazed nose section seriously hampered night operations and so, on the recommendation of the Fighter Interception Unit (FIU), much of this was blanked off on the nightfighter variants. BAe

The Bristol Beaufighter was the first truly effective nightfighter in RAF service. Its prototype — R2052 illustrated — first flew on 17 July 1939 and production aircraft became available in the summer of 1940. By the time the night Blitz ended in May 1941 a total of 200 had been completed. BAe

In April 1940 the Fighter Interception Unit (FIU) was formed at Tangmere to work on the development of night-fighting tactics and techniques. Although much concerned with bringing the AI radar equipment to a state of operational proficiency, this was by no means its only responsibility. It also examined the varying conditions of visibility during darkness and advised on the best ways of approaching the target. Another problem tackled by FIU was that of reflected glare from the searchlights reducing Blenheim pilots' night vision. The Unit experimented with various panels of the aircraft's extensively-glazed nose section blanked off until it arrived at the best compromise to reduce reflections without seriously impairing visibility. Ground control procedures were evaluated and various improvements worked out. One useful recommendation was that standard radius turns be adopted by the nightfighter squadrons, so that the controller's job of bringing the Blenheim and its quarry together could be carried out more precisely. All of this work reduced the burden on the frontline nightfighter squadrons and, since unusually for a development unit the FIU flew on actual operations, its recommendations were always eminently practical. Commanded by Wg Cdr G. P. Chamberlain, the Unit was initially equipped with six Blenheims fitted with AI Mk II. It was to remain in being for the remainder of the war and became extremely influential in the development of night-fighting tactics. From March 1940 the work of the scientists, the operational trials units and the frontline squadrons was co-ordinated by the Air Ministry's Night Interception Committee, which worked under the direction of the Deputy Chief of the Air Staff.

Although the Blenheim If had become the RAF's principal specialised nightfighter aircraft by default, rather than through any particular suitability for the role, it did appear to offer an adequate, if not entirely satisfactory operational platform for the first air interception radar to be used in combat. The aircraft's poor performance and manoeuvrability had led to its relegation to nightfighter work and its speed was further reduced by the drag of the AI aerials when radar was installed. The original Blenheim I bomber's armament of one fixed, forward-firing .303in machine gun and a second .303in weapon in a dorsal turret, had been augmented in the Blenheim If by a ventral pack of four .303in Browning machine guns. Thus weight of fire was little more than half that of the RAF's

standard dayfighters, with their batteries of eight .303in Brownings. Yet, the Blenheim did provide adequate space for the radar operator and his equipment. By mid-1940 a total of 31 Blenheim Ifs fitted with AI Mk III were in service. The AI Mk III was the first production model air interception radar, but reliability was poor and both operators and servicing technicians were perforce inexperienced. The radar's transmitter aerial was fitted in the Blenheim's nose, with azimuth receiver aerials on the engine nacelles and elevation receiver aerials above and below the port wing. It was intended that all six of Fighter Command's Blenheim squadrons (Nos 23, 25, 29, 219, 600 and 604) should become AI-equipped, pending availability of the more suitable Bristol Beaufighter. However, operational experience with the Blenheim If nightfighters during June 1940 was so disappointing that it seemed as though the single-seat dayfighters would provide a better night defence. It was not until the end of August 1940 that the Defiant turret fighters were switched from day- to night-fighting and it proved to be difficult (although ultimately not impossible) to fit them with AI. The Douglas DB-7 bombers diverted from French orders, which began to arrive in Britain during that summer, were more easily converted as radar-equipped nightfighters, when they were known as Havocs. However, like the Blenheims, they too were deficient in performance and

fire-power. So the only immediately available alternatives to the Blenheim If for night operations were the Hurricane and Spitfire.

The Luftwaffe began small-scale night raiding against targets in Britain on 5 June 1940 and these continued intermittently throughout the month. RAF nightfighters engaged enemy bombers on 21 occasions and 11 of them fell to the defences, with one bomber falling to AA fire. None of these victories was gained by AI-equipped Blenheims, honours being divided between single-seat fighters and Blenheims lacking radar flying 'Cat's Eyes' patrols. And, on the debit side, Fighter Command lost six Blenheims, three Hurricanes and a Spitfire during night operations. Moreover, the defenders' success was due in large measure to faulty German tactics. Most of the bombers flew at altitudes between 8,000 and 12,000ft, where the searchlights were able to pick them up without much difficulty. Depending as they did on an antiquated sound location system, the searchlights were easily defeated by increasing the bombers' operating altitudes to heights above 17,000ft at which sound location became ineffective. And, without searchlight illumination, 'Cat's Eyes' patrols became even more chancey affairs — for if a target could be held in the searchlight's beam, it was visible from a distance of some five miles and the dayfighter command and control system was capable of bringing a defender to within this distance. However, without the assistance of the searchlights, greater precision in fighter direction was required and the existing control system simply could not bring the defender to within the necessary range. Even an AI-equipped fighter required ground control to within 3 miles of the target. The June 1940 night interceptions highlighted other faults in the control system. Controllers tended to think it sufficient to direct the nightfighter into the general vicinity of the enemy aircraft and leave the pilot to carry out a visual search as best he could. Instead, it was necessary for the nightfighter to be positioned below and astern of the enemy by the controller's instructions. Similarly, it should be the controller's responsibility to track the nightfighter and he should not, as was often the case, expect the pilot to report his precise position. The latter had many more pressing matters to occupy his attention. It was also found that both Group and Sector control rooms could become overloaded when there was comparatively heavy night activity. All that could be done in such instances was to order nightfighters on standing patrol along predetermined lines, in the hope that they would encounter enemy aircraft. By the end of June it was clear that the dayfighters' command and control system was quite inadequate for the direction of nightfighters. An entirely new arrangement was necessary.

The activities of four RAF squadrons on the night of 18/19 June 1940 give a good idea of the character of nightfighter operations at this period. It was a night of quite widespread German bomber activity, with bombs falling on Addington (the first in the Greater London area) and Cambridge, where nine people were killed. No 74 Squadron, a Spitfire dayfighter unit, was based at Rochford near Southend. Seeing enemy bombers held by searchlight beams in the vicinity, they obtained the controller's permission to send up a single Spitfire. It was flown by the redoubtable Flt Lt A. G. 'Sailor' Malan. Immediately after take-off, he sighted a He111 held in searchlight beams at 8,000ft and heading for the coast; climbing up in pursuit, Malan got astern of the enemy aircraft. He opened fire at 200yd range, closing to 50yd and firing a single long burst. He saw his bullets hit and the Spitfire's windscreen was covered with oil from the enemy bomber. As the He111 spiralled out of the searchlight beam, Malan broke off the attack. Seeing a second He111 held by searchlights at 12,000ft, Malan went after it; he got into position 250yd astern and, matching his speed with that of the bomber, fired two five-second bursts. The enemy bomber dived down to crash in flames near Chelmsford. Both of these He111s were assessed as confirmed destroyed. Another Spitfire unit, No 19 Squadron based at Duxford, was in action that night. Flg Off P. G. Petre engaged an enemy bomber held by searchlights but, as he opened the attack, his own aircraft was hit by return fire. Petre baled out, but was badly burned on the face and hands. A second German bomber was later attacked by Flg Off G. E. Ball and this crashed near Margate. These two combats were the squadron's only encounter with the enemy during the month, although a total of 20 night patrols were flown between 8 June and 28 June.

The fortunes of two Blenheim squadrons were rather more mixed on that night of 18/19 June.

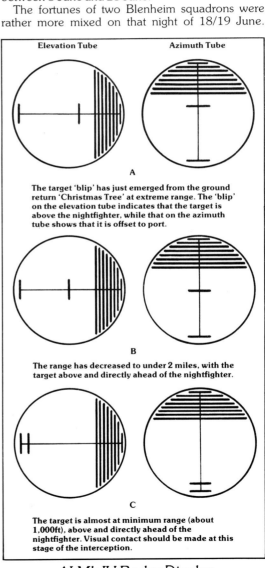

Elevation Tube   **Azimuth Tube**

A

The target 'blip' has just emerged from the ground return 'Christmas Tree' at extreme range. The 'blip' on the elevation tube indicates that the target is above the nightfighter, while that on the azimuth tube shows that it is offset to port.

B

The range has decreased to under 2 miles, with the target above and directly ahead of the nightfighter.

C

The target is almost at minimum range (about 1,000ft), above and directly ahead of the nightfighter. Visual contact should be made at this stage of the interception.

AI Mk IV Radar Display

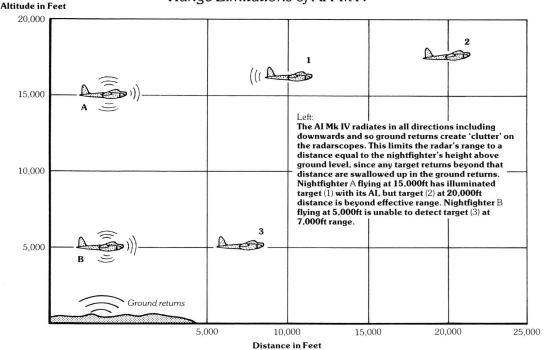

Altitude in Feet

20,000

15,000

A

10,000

5,000

B

Ground returns

1

2

3

Left:
The AI Mk IV radiates in all directions including downwards and so ground returns create 'clutter' on the radarscopes. This limits the radar's range to a distance equal to the nightfighter's height above ground level, since any target returns beyond that distance are swallowed up in the ground returns. Nightfighter A flying at 15,000ft has illuminated target (1) with its AI, but target (2) at 20,000ft distance is beyond effective range. Nightfighter B flying at 5,000ft is unable to detect target (3) at 7,000ft range.

5,000   10,000   15,000   20,000   25,000

Distance in Feet

No 23 Squadron, based at Collyweston, Northants, sent up seven Blenheims on patrol and three of them made contact with enemy aircraft. That flown by Sgt Close was approaching a He111 when it was hit by the bomber's defensive fire. Close was killed, but his air gunner escaped by parachute before the Blenheim crashed. Plt Off R. M. Duke-Woolley, on patrol near King's Lynn, saw Close's Blenheim go down and pursued the German bomber. He caught it over the coast and, after firing two bursts into it, saw the He111 go down to crash near Sheringham. The squadron's third combat of the night took place near Newmarket. Sqn Ldr J. O'Brien saw a He111 illuminated by searchlights and positioned his Blenheim beneath it, giving his dorsal gunner the chance to open the attack. After several bursts of fire, the enemy aircraft turned to port and dived; O'Brien then continued the attack with his forward-firing guns. The He111's starboard engine began to smoke and it went down to crash. Shortly afterwards, O'Brien lost control of the Blenheim and it fell in a spin. The pilot ordered his crew to bale out, but only he managed to get clear before the aircraft crashed. No 29 Squadron based at Debden, fought two combats — Plt Off J. D. Humphries exchanged fire with a He111 over Bury St Edmunds. Both aircraft were hit: the German bomber's port engine being damaged and the Blenheim's hydraulic system knocked out. The two combatants separated, honours even. Later that

night, Plt Off J. S. Barnwell, son of the aircraft designer F. S. Barnwell, engaged a He111, which was seen to go down in flames. However, Barnwell's Blenheim failed to return and was presumed to have crashed in the sea.

The long-awaited first victory for an AI Blenheim came on the night of 22/23 July. Flg Off G. Ashfield of the FIU was on patrol over the Sussex coast when he was alerted by Poling Chain Home radar station to the presence of enemy aircraft and directed into position to intercept. The Blenheim's radar operator, Sgt R. Leyland, picked up a contact at a range of 1 mile and as the distance closed Ashfield was able to spot the enemy aircraft, a Dornier Do17; his fire sent it down to crash burning, into the sea. The teething troubles with the AI radar were far from over, although Ashfield's victory gave cause for hope. Moreover, the improved AI Mk IV began its trials that summer. However, a reliable AI radar could not by itself provide the answer to the night interception problem. This, as we have seen, also depended on the provision of a satisfactory command and control system. No radar system was available for inland tracking, the Chain Home stations being for early-warning. Once a daylight raider had crossed the coast, it was reported by the Observer Corps posts with generally satisfactory accuracy. Yet by night the Observers could only rely on sound plots, which were good enough for air raid warning purposes, but far too imprecise to be used for control of interceptions. The answer was a ground-based radar tracking system, which could be used to bring the nightfighter into close enough range to the enemy aircraft for its own AI to acquire the target. The necessary radar equipment, known as GCI (ground control of interception), was quickly devised and six sets were ordered under the highest priority, with delivery required by the end of the year.

The development of GCI allowed far more accurate control of the interception than was possible under the earlier system. This was because the controller worked directly from a radar screen, which showed the relative positions of both target and nightfighter. Using the dayfighter control system, information from various sources was plotted on an operations table from which the controller obtained the positions of nightfighter and quarry. The enemy aircraft's position was reported by the radar early warning stations and, after crossing the coast, by Observer Corps sound plots, whereas that of the RAF nightfighter was obtained by high-frequency radio direction-finding. As the operations room plot was built up from different sources, it was likely to incorporate various minor errors — for example, time lags between obtaining and reporting information and minor inaccuracies in position reporting. None of these made much difference in daylight. However, at night it frequently happened that the controller directed the nightfighter into a position which corresponded exactly with that of the enemy aircraft on the

Height in Feet

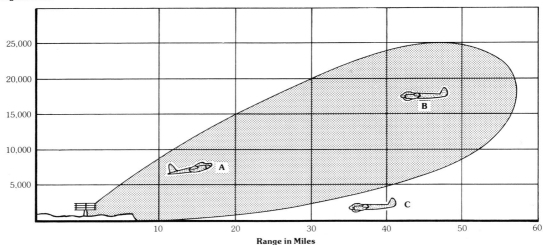

GCI Radar Coverage

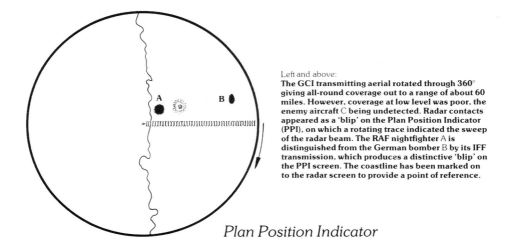

Left and above:
The GCI transmitting aerial rotated through 360° giving all-round coverage out to a range of about 60 miles. However, coverage at low level was poor, the enemy aircraft C being undetected. Radar contacts appeared as a 'blip' on the Plan Position Indicator (PPI), on which a rotating trace indicated the sweep of the radar beam. The RAF nightfighter A is distinguished from the German bomber B by its IFF transmission, which produces a distinctive 'blip' on the PPI screen. The coastline has been marked on to the radar screen to provide a point of reference.

Plan Position Indicator

operations room plot, but the RAF aircraft's AI was unable to pick up a target within range. Very accurate information on the relative position of target and nightfighter was therefore essential in nightfighter control, and this the GCI provided. The radar gave a 360° coverage over a range of some 50 miles, but initially was unable to provide information on the height of contacts. Nonetheless, it represented a tremendous advance in nightfighter control, hence the urgency to get it into service.

During the six months or so which elapsed between the placing of orders for the first GCI sets and the equipment coming into use, an experimental radar-controlled night interception system was in operation in the Kenley Sector. As German bombers which made their landfall over Beachy Head usually passed through this Sector en route to London, it was well placed for such trials. However, despite numerous contacts being made, the outcome was ultimately disappointing. The Kenley experiment made use of 10 GL or gun-laying radars loaned from the Army. These had been developed for the direction of AA fire and had a slant range of about 40,000ft and gave height estimates to within an accuracy of 1,000ft. The GL radars were installed at searchlight posts and their contacts were passed by telephone to the Sector operations room, where they were plotted on a gridded blackboard.

However, since the fighter's position was determined by radio direction-finding, there remained some of the problems of the day control system and plots from enemy aircraft and nightfighters were sometimes confused. The main method of nightfighter direction was radio-telephone communication from the sector controller, but searchlights were also used. For, although their beams were unable to illuminate the target, they could at least provide a pointer towards the position of the enemy aircraft. The nightfighters, operating from the satellite airfield at Redhill, included a number of the new Beaufighters which were just coming into service. However, AI-equipped Blenheims carried out most of the patrols and this type's slowness and weak firepower was one of the reasons why the Kenley experiment failed to achieve much success against the German raiders. The much faster and better-armed Beaufighters suffered from the teething problems inseparable from the introduction of a new aircraft into service. Furthermore, the

Below:
The Beaufighter's main armament comprised four 20mm Hispano cannon mounted in the underside of the nose, the starboard pair being illustrated below. In addition, it carried six wing-mounted .303in machine guns. BAe

airfield at Redhill, which had only just been taken over by Fighter Command in September 1940, was in several ways unsuitable for nightfighter operations: it was a grass airfield and was prone to become waterlogged; maintenance facilities were primitive, and dampness and maintenance problems combined to exacerbate the already temperamental behaviour of the nightfighters' delicate electrical equipment. Yet, at the height of the Battle of Britain, no other airfield could be found for the nightfighters in the Kenley Sector. No 600 Squadron began operations from Redhill in September, but they were soon replaced by No 219 Squadron, which remained there until December. Although these trials in radar-controlled night-fighting showed great promise for the future, the actual results were poor. Yet Dowding was impressed by the work of No 219 Squadron (commanded by Sqn Ldr J. H. Little DFC) which he reported 'operated with great energy and enthusiasm under extremely adverse and difficult conditions'.

The need for an efficient night air defence system became an altogether more serious and pressing problem in late August 1940, when the Luftwaffe began heavy night raiding. And this was but a prelude to the full-scale night Blitz to which the entire bomber forces of three *Luftflotten* were committed at the end of September. It was of course Fighter Command's victory in the daylight fighting of the Battle of Britain which had led to this change in strategy by the German High Command. Yet it forced on that Command's nightfighter squadrons a trial of strength which they were not then ready to meet. Fortunately, the nightfighters were not Britain's only means of defence against night attack, although ultimately they proved to be the most effective. The Luftwaffe's reliance on blind bombing beams opened up possibilities of radio countermeasures, which were to be brilliantly exploited. The guns and searchlights of the Army's Anti-Aircraft Command had a powerful influence on the morale of attackers and defenders alike, even though the material results of their efforts were not great. Deception techniques, such as the 'Starfish' site's decoy fires intended to attract German bombs, also played their part. But, ultimately, Britain's strongest line of defence in the Blitz was its people's firm will to resist, which was inspired and memorably articulated by the Prime Minister, Winston Churchill.

At the beginning of September 1940 there were only eight specialised nightfighter squadrons. They comprised the six Blenheim If squadrons, which were to receive their first Beaufighters that month, and the two Defiant squadrons (No 141 and No 264) relegated from day-fighting duties. In addition the FIU at Tangmere was able to carry out limited operations, its strength being much less than a properly constituted squadron. These forces could, in theory at least, be augmented by the aircraft of the dayfighter squadrons. However, not only were most of these units still heavily committed to the day battle, but few of them had any useful experience of night operations. There were, however, exceptions: the Hurricane-equipped No 73 Squadron had trained for night-fighting in addition to its day-fighting commitments after returning from France in June 1940. It was declared operational by night early in August and in September moved to the Debden satellite of Castle Camps for night patrols over London. No 92 Squadron, flying Spitfires, had carried out night patrols from Pembrey and Bibury during July and August in defence of South Wales and the industrial

RAF Nightfighter Squadrons November 1940		
Squadron	Aircraft	Base
No 23 Squadron	Blenheim If	Ford
No 25 Squadron	Blenheim If; Beaufighter If	Debden
No 29 Squadron	Blenheim If	Wittering; Digby
No 73 Squadron	Hurricane I	Castle Camps
No 85 Squadron	Hurricane I	Kirton-in-Lindsey; Caistor
No 87 Squadron (B Flight)	Hurricane I	Bibury
No 141 Squadron	Defiant I	Gatwick
No 151 Squadron	Hurricane I	Digby
No 219 Squadron	Blenheim If; Beaufighter If	Redhill
No 264 Squadron	Defiant	Rochford
No 600 Squadron	Blenheim If	Catterick; Drem
No 604 Squadron	Blenheim If	Middle Wallop
Fighter Interception Unit	Blenheim If	Tangmere

Midlands. In return for the loss of two Spitfires destroyed and three damaged, one He111 fell to the guns of Flg Off A. R. Wright. However, on 8 September the Squadron moved to Biggin Hill and immediately became embroiled in the day battle, so that its expertise was lost to the night defences. Since late July, No 87 Squadron's Hurricanes had also flown night patrols on a regular basis. Each flight was alternatively detached from its main base at Church Fenton to Hullavington and Bibury for this duty.

With the War Cabinet's attention so forcibly directed to the question of night air defence, in early September the Air Council decided to set up a special committee to give urgent attention to the nightfighter's problems. It was chaired by the former Chief of the Air Staff, Marshal of the RAF Sir John Salmond and its members included such distinguished air officers as Freeman, Joubert, Tedder and Sholto Douglas. The committee made four recommendations: that a specialised nightfighter operational training unit (OTU) be set up; that prospective nightfighter pilots undergo a rigorous night vision test; that a special nightfighter staff be organised at Headquarters Fighter Command; and that navigational aids be provided for nightfighters. These were all eminently sensible suggestions, although none could be implemented in time to affect the present crisis. Moreover, Fighter Command's hard-pressed staff officers, who were well

aware of the problems and were doing their utmost to meet them, somewhat resented this unsolicited advice from on high. More controversially, the Salmond Committee suggested that at least one dayfighter squadron should be re-assigned to nightfighter work. Dowding resisted this move, arguing that only radar-equipped nightfighters would be able to achieve systematic and consistent results by night. Although — as we have seen — his position was not a dogmatic one, and several dayfighter units had already achieved a degree of specialisation in night-fighting. Significantly, Sholto Douglas was the main proponent of the Salmond Committee's argument, this debate having parallels with the better known 'Big Wings' controversy over dayfighter tactics. Dowding was overruled by the Air Staff and he was ordered to convert three Hurricane dayfighter squadrons to the night-fighting role. After Dowding was unceremoniously relieved of his Command in November 1940, it was Sholto Douglas who took over as AOC-in-C Fighter Command. Yet Dowding, the architect of Britain's air defences, was to have the last word in this

Below:
In November 1940 No 87 Squadron became a specialised nightfighter unit, one of three Hurricane units so designated at that time. The photograph shows the squadron's CO Sqn Ldr Ian Gleed, bringing his Hurricane I in to land. IWM

particular debate: writing in 1941 he foresaw the
time when *every* fighter would be fitted with AI —
and history was to vindicate his prescience.

The desperate days of the Blitz called forth some
unconventional solutions to the problems of night
defence; none were more bizarre than the idea of
an aerial minefield. A string of aerial mines,
suspended from parachutes was to be dropped in
the path of the approaching bombers, in the hope
of bringing large numbers of them down. Perhaps
because the idea had the support of Churchill's
scientific adviser Prof F. A. Lindemann, it was
actually implemented using obsolete Handley Page
Harrow bombers as aerial minelayers. As Fighter
Command's experts had predicted from the outset,
the project, codenamed 'Mutton', was a dismal
failure. In order to have a chance of succeeding, the
minelaying aircraft had to be placed in exactly the
right position ahead of the incoming bombers. And
if Fighter Command had the means of doing this, it
could be used to better effect in positioning
nightfighters. The crux of the night defence problem
was in accurately determining the position of the
target, not in bringing the bomber down after it had
been located. A somewhat better-conceived,
although ultimately unsuccessful, project was the
airborne searchlight or Turbinlite, which was the
brainchild of Wg Cdr W. Helmore. Fitted in the
nose of a modified Havoc aircraft, which carried AI
radar, the searchlight would illuminate a target for
accompanying Hurricanes to attack. It was 1942
before this equipment went into squadron service,
but the difficulties of co-ordinating the efforts of the
aircraft which carried the detection equipment with
that carrying the armament proved to be insur-
mountable.

On becoming the new AOC-in-C Fighter
Command on 25 November, AM Sir William Sholto
Douglas determined to expand the nightfighter
force to a strength of 20 squadrons. However, as
deliveries of the new twin-engined Beaufighter and
Havoc nightfighters were slow, and trained crews
were in short supply, this objective proved
impossible to achieve before the end of the Blitz.
Other improvements to the night defences were
being implemented, though. No 54 OTU had been
formed at Church Fenton to give specialist training
to nightfighter crews. The facilities at nightfighter
airfields were much improved by the provision of
radar homing beacons, blind approach radars and
meteorological officers, all which helped to reduce
the hazards of operating in darkness. In addition,
procedures were devised to allow AI-equipped
nightfighters and the Hurricane and Defiant 'Cat's
Eyes' fighters to operate at the same time, without
interfering with each other's efforts. This was
achieved by assigning the 'Cat's Eyes' fighters to
patrol lines over the target area, allocating each a
separate height band and restricting AA fire to lower
altitudes. The radar-directed nightfighters operated
over the coast and the target's approaches.

The three Hurricane units allocated to specialised
night defence duties were Nos 73, 85 and 151
Squadrons. The latter unit, its illustrious record in
World War 1 notwithstanding, had no recent
night-fighting experience and nor had No 85
Squadron. Inexplicably, No 73 Squadron's specialised skills in this role were lost to Fighter Command
in November, when it was posted to the Middle East
as a dayfighter unit. No 87 Squadron took its place.
Dowding was not alone in doubting the suitability of
the Hurricane for night-fighting: the Commanding
Officer of No 85 Squadron, Sqn Ldr P. W. Towns-
end identified many shortcomings in the fighter for

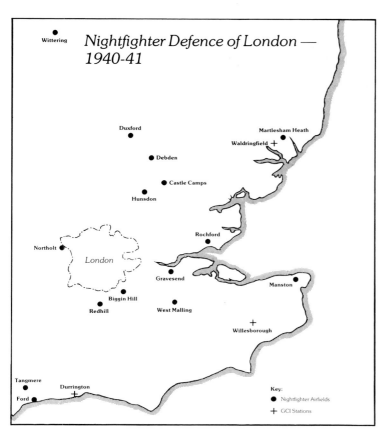

Nightfighter Defence of London — 1940-41

Wittering

Duxford

Martlesham Heath

Waldringfield +

Debden

Castle Camps

Hunsdon

Rochford

Northolt

London

Gravesend

Manston

Biggin Hill

Redhill

West Malling

Willesborough +

Tangmere

Durrington +

Ford

Key:

● Nightfighter Airfields

+ GCI Stations

Left:
Hurricane IIc fighters of No 3 Squadron co-operated with the Turbinlite Havocs of No 1451 Flight, but achieved no success in this role. The Hurricanes also carried out 'Cat's Eyes' night patrols and Intruder sorties over France. BAe

the new role, including its comparatively poor endurance, lack of exhaust anti-glare shields, cramped cockpit and inefficient instrument panel lighting. The results of the squadron's first night combats tended to confirm these assertions. On 27/28 October, Flt Lt G. Allard, a highly experienced and successful dayfighter pilot operating from Kirton-in-Lindsey, intercepted an enemy aircraft which was attacking two RAF machines showing navigation lights. All he could see was his opponent's exhaust flames, but using them as a reference he was able to position the Hurricane for an attack from astern. Allard fired two short bursts, but was blinded by his own tracers and so lost

Left:
No 247 Squadron's Hurricane IIcs were teamed with the Turbinlite Havocs of No 1457 Flight, which formed at Colerne in September 1941 and moved to the Hurricanes' airfield at Predannack two months later. BAe

Below:
No 73 Squadron was one of Fighter Command's most experienced Hurricane night-fighter units when in November 1940 it was despatched to the Middle East in the dayfighter role. However, it subsequently reverted to night operations in its new theatre. IWM OM1228

contact with the enemy aircraft. The following night Sgt G. Goodman encountered a German raider. Before he could make visual contact, he was sighted by the enemy gunner, who opened fire on the Hurricane. Using the German tracers as a reference, Goodman fired three bursts in return. He then saw the indistinct shape of his opponent, but it disappeared into cloud before he could resume the attack.

The approach of winter compounded the problems of the 'Cat's Eyes' fighters, which unlike the twin-engined nightfighters, had no reliable navigation aids. Nonetheless, some successful combats were recorded. The two Defiant units were operating from airfields adjacent to the Thames Estuary — No 141 Squadron at Gravesend and No 264 Squadron at Rochford. It was intended to form two nightfighter wings (each two squadrons strong) at these bases to cover one of the approach routes to London. However, when 'A' Flight of No 85 Squadron attempted to move to Gravesend in early November, it was found that there was no accommodation for it. The problem was later resolved and the whole squadron moved to Gravesend on 23 November. Plt Off F. D. Hughes of No 264 Squadron, who had gained his first night victory on 15/16 October, had a frustrating encounter with a He111 on 23/24 November. He was directed by the controller to intercept a bandit

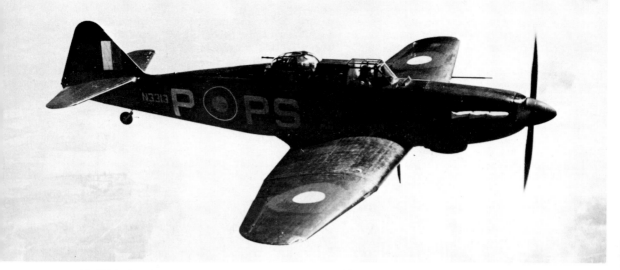

at 12,000ft, but then, seeing a searchlight cone to starboard and 4,000ft higher, he climbed up to investigate. Hughes' gunner, Sgt F. Gash, spotted the exhaust of the enemy bomber shortly afterwards above and ahead of the Defiant. Hughes closed in and at 250yd range Gash opened fire: the opening burst found its mark and the He111 lost speed. When within less than 100yd of the bomber, Gash fired two more bursts, but he was blinded by the muzzle flash from his four .303in Brownings. At that point the turret jammed. Hughes skilfully obtained one more hit on the He111, by hosing the tracer from the turret guns on to the target. The enemy bomber was last seen going down towards the sea and was claimed as probably destroyed.

As Hughes' combat showed, courage and determination could sometimes go some way towards redeeming deficiencies in equipment. One pilot with a large measure of both qualities was Plt Off R. P. Stevens, a Hurricane pilot of No 151

Squadron. His wife and children had been killed in a bombing raid and so for him night combat was a matter of personal vengeance. He opened his account with the enemy on 15 January 1941, shooting down two bombers — his squadron's first night victories of World War 2. By the end of the Blitz in May, he had claimed 10 enemy aircraft destroyed, by far the highest claim for a nightfighter pilot at that time. He failed to return from an intruder sortie on 15 December 1941.

The first Beaufighter night victory went to Flt Lt John Cunningham and radar operator Sgt J.

Phillipson of No 604 Squadron on 19/ 20 November 1940. With a maximum speed of 320mph (compared with the Blenheim's beggarly 225mph), the Beaufighter marked a tremendous improvement in night-fighting capability. Its armament of four 20mm cannon and six .303in machine guns was the heaviest of any RAF fighter at that time and it carried the AI Mk IV radar, which was better both in performance and reliability than the earlier AI sets. The radar operators too were gaining in skill, as men of the right aptitude were selected for this duty. Early recruitment for this highly-specialised duty had at first been haphazard and many unsuitable operators had struggled unavail-ingly to master the early AI equipment. It was found that a high mathematical ability was generally desirable, although by no means all successful Radio Operators (ROs) as they were officially known conformed in this respect. One of their least welcome duties on the early Beaufighters was changing the cannon ammunition drums in combat.

Above:
The AI Mk IV radar installation in the Beaufighter If included a nose-mounted, dipole transmitter aerial and wing-mounted receiver aerials. Operating on a frequency of 1½m, the radar was effective in detecting targets at medium altitudes. BAe

Before a belt-feed system was introduced, the 20mm cannon were fed by 60-round ammunition drums. This meant leaving his AI set — and oxygen supply — to fumble in darkness with the heavy drums, often in a manoeuvring aircraft.

The control of night interceptions underwent a similar radical improvement in January 1941, when the first six GCI stations became operational, and by April that year there were 11 of them in service; controllers worked from the radar sites, rather than as previously from operations rooms. Their main source of information was the Plan Position Indicator (PPI), which gave a plan view of the area swept by the radar. A trace revolved around the

screen with each sweep of the radar aerial and any contact would appear as a 'blip' of light. The Identification Friend or Foe (IFF) transmitter carried by every RAF aircraft produced a distinctive return, which enabled the hunter to be easily distinguished from the quarry. As the height-finding ability of the early GCI radars was poor, they usually worked in conjunction with GL radars which were more accurate in determining altitude. Although very sophisticated in concept, the early GCI stations were makeshift affairs — a visitor described 'a few wooden huts . . . a caravan draped in a tarpaulin and a strange contraption which looked more like a huge flattened birdcage than an aerial array'. Amazingly, the aerial was rotated by two airmen operating a bicycle-like pedal contraption.

AI Mk IV fitted in Beaufighters, working with the new GCI radars soon began to show results, although progress was steady rather than spectacular. A typical night interception was carried out by Flt Lt G. O. Budd of No 604 Squadron on 10/11 April 1941. Operating with Sopley GCI, he was directed on to a bandit and his radar operator, Sgt Evans, picked up a contact on his AI at 3,000ft

RAF Nightfighter Squadrons May 1941

Squadron	Aircraft	Base
No 25 Squadron	Beaufighter If	Wittering
No 29 Squadron	Beaufighter If	West Malling
No 68 Squadron	Blenheim If; Beaufighter If	High Ercall
No 85 Squadron	Havoc I	Hunsdon
No 87 Squadron	Hurricane I	Charmy Down
No 93 Squadron	Harrow (aerial minelaying)	Middle Wallop
No 96 Squadron	Defiant I; Hurricane I	Cranage
No 141 Squadron	Defiant I	Acklington; Ayr
No 151 Squadron	Defiant I	Wittering
No 219 Squadron	Beaufighter If	Tangmere
No 255 Squadron	Defiant If; Hurricane I	Kirton-in-Lindsey
No 256 Squadron	Defiant I; Hurricane I	Squire's Gate
No 264 Squadron	Defiant I	West Malling; Nutt's Corner
No 307 Squadron	Defiant I	Exeter
No 600 Squadron	Beaufighter If	Colerne
No 604 Squadron	Beaufighter If	Middle Wallop
Fighter Interception Unit	Beaufighter If	Ford

Note: No 23 Squadron engaged on Intruder operations, but available for night air defence in an emergency

range. Budd closed in below the German bomber, which he identified as a He111 and opened fire at between 200 and 150yd range. The enemy aircraft caught fire and then broke up in mid-air. The Beaufighter crew then went on to gain a second victory that night. However, one disadvantage of the GCI system was already apparent and this was its limited capacity. As a station could only control one nightfighter at a time, it easily became saturated during a raid. A cab-rank system was instituted to ensure that, as one interception was completed, a second Beaufighter was available for direction. Even so, there were usually more nightfighters airborne than could be controlled and so freelance patrols were begun. By using searchlights as an indication of the general location of enemy aircraft, crews could sometimes pick up a contact on their AI sets without the help of ground control.

The general improvements in night-fighting techniques were seen in the results obtained between January and May 1941. In January 486 sorties produced only 11 contacts and three enemy aircraft destroyed. February was little better, with only four nightfighter victories, but March saw an improvement. Over 1,000 sorties were flown, producing 56 contacts and 22 victories. An increased sortie rate in April resulted in claims for 48 enemy bombers, while a peak effort in May of 1,988 night sorties resulted in 96 victories. Although these victories were divided fairly evenly between 'Cat's Eyes' and AI fighters, the latter had flown less than half the number of sorties carried out by the single-engined fighters and had gained twice as many contacts. It was a clear pointer to the future. Yet, the achievement must be seen in perspective: the nightfighters' victories represented an attrition rate of under 4% of the German bombers' sorties, which was an acceptable loss rate.

The Blitz ended in May 1941 when the greater part of the Luftwaffe's bomber force moved east for the campaign against the Soviet Union. Sholto Douglas was confident that, had the night offensive continued, Fighter Command would have defeated it. Be that as it may, it is certain that his predecessor Dowding had laid sound foundations for a radar-directed night defence system. By that time 15 specialised nightfighter squadrons were operational and seven of them were flying AI-equipped fighters. Conversion of six Blenheim squadrons to Beaufighters was well advanced and the first Havocs were in service with No 85 Squadron. The RAF's night defences had come far from the early days of haphazard 'Cat's Eyes' patrols.

Below:
As an insurance against possible supply problems with the Bristol Hercules radial engine, the Merlin-engined Beaufighter IIf was produced. A total of 450 of this mark was built and 10 nightfighter squadrons flew Beaufighters IIfs. BAe

Major Night Attacks on Britain January-May 1941					
Month	No of Raids	German Sorties	Defensive Sorties	Nightfighter Detection	Combats	Claims
January	14	1,444	486	78	11	3
February	2	125	568	58	13	4
March	19	3,128	1,005	149	56	22
April	21	3,983	1,184	172	94	48
May	15	2,441	1,988	371	196	96

3 Intruders

Intruding, essentially the offensive employment of nightfighters, was pioneered by the Blenheim Ifs of No 600 Squadron and No 604 Squadron during June 1940, following the precedent set by No 151 Squadron during World War 1. The Luftwaffe's nightfighters were also to exploit this method of operations during 1940-41, although thereafter they largely abandoned it in favour of purely defensive night-fighting. By contrast, the RAF steadily expanded its Intruder effort, so that by the final months of the war Intruders were routinely operating throughout the length and breadth of German territory. The Intruders' primary targets were bomber and nightfighter aircraft operating over their own airfields. Indeed, the battle against the Luftwaffe's nightfighter forces was to be extended by the Bomber Support squadrons of No 100 Group to the point where the German aircraft could be detected and attacked at any time during their missions and not just at take-off and landing. However, Intruders could also attack certain other targets, such as railway locomotives,

when opportunity offered. And, early in 1943, freelance night-fighting patrols known as 'Night Rangers' were begun to supplement the more carefully planned and less flexible Intruder missions.

In December 1940 the RAF decided to assign one of its Blenheim nightfighter squadrons to specialist Intruder duties. No 23 Squadron was selected, being replaced by No 68 Squadron for defensive night-fighting. Its Blenheims were stripped of AI radar equipment, as this could not be risked over enemy territory. In addition to the standard gun arrangement, the Blenheim Mk 1fs carried bombs for airfield attacks and flares for illumination. Their patrols were not haphazard, but were intended to cover airfields at which RAF Intelligence anticipated night-bomber activity. A

Above:
No 23 Squadron was the pioneer night Intruder unit in the RAF operating the Blenheim If. It began operations over Northern France in December 1940 and gained its first victory on 2 January 1941. MoD

primary source of information was radio intercepts from the Y-Service and by late 1940 the 'Ultra' codebreakers were reading the Luftwaffe's Enigma cyphers. Operations began on 21/22 December with six Intruder patrols over the Abbeville, Amiens and Poix areas. But, although four German aircraft were sighted and bombs dropped on six airfields, no definite results were claimed. On the following night the squadron flew seven sorties, again without apparent effect, although one of its own aircraft was lost. This Blenheim ran out of fuel on its return flight and the crew took to their parachutes over the Isle of Wight. The success of Intruder operations could not simply be measured in terms of the losses

inflicted, however, as the harrying of enemy bombers over their own airfields was intended to exert psychological pressures on their crews.

On 2/3 January 1941 a Blenheim If flown by Flg Off P. Ensor encountered a German bomber over Caen. It had its navigation lights burning and so was easily trailed. Ensor followed it to the vicinity of Dreux, hoping to surprise the German bomber on its approach to land when it would be most vulnerable. However, as the Blenheim was running

Below:
In April 1941 No 23 Squadron began to operate the Havoc I — an adaptation of the Douglas Boston light bomber — in the Intruder role. Forward-firing armament comprised four .303in machine guns and a bomb-load of 2,400lb could be carried. Illustrated is BD121:F which was later transferred to the Fleet Air Arm. IWM CH2786

low on fuel, he then decided to attack. On closing in to 100yd, Ensor recognised the target as a He111. After the Blenheim's opening burst of fire, an explosion occurred in the Heinkel's rear fuselage. The German bomber fired off recognition flares, obviously assuming that it was being attacked by a friendly aircraft in error. Ensor followed up his opening attack with a second burst of fire, exhausting his ammunition in the process. The He111 was last seen diving away, apparently out of control. Another successful Intruder pilot at this time was Flt Lt B. R. O'Bryen Hoare, who was later to command No 23 Squadron. Having claimed a probable victory on 3/4 March, he made certain of his second victim on the night of 21/22 April. Hoare took off from Manston and set course for the airfield at Achiet, which he had been briefed to patrol. But, seeing a lighted flarepath at Douai, he elected to attack this; he dropped four bombs across the airfield, causing the lights to be extinguished. He then flew on to St Leger which was also illuminated, and sighted two aircraft with recognition lights burning in the landing pattern. The first of these got

down safely before the Blenheim could reach it, so Hoare positioned the Blenheim astern of the second. This he reported as a large four-engined aircraft and it was probably a Focke-Wulf Fw200 Condor of I/KG40. Hoare opened fire from close range and saw the German aircraft explode and disintegrate in the air, fragments from it hitting the Blenheim.

This combat was to be No 23 Squadron's last success with the Blenheim, as its replacement with the Douglas Havoc was by then almost complete. Performance and handling of the new aircraft were an improvement over the Blenheim and a bomb-load of 2,400lb could be carried. However, the forward-firing armament of four .303in machine guns was clearly inadequate and this was to be improved with later variants. The first Havoc Intruder sortie was flown on 7/8 April by No 23 Squadron's Commanding Officer, Wg Cdr G. F. W. Heycock, and during the following month six combats with enemy aircraft were recorded. The Havocs' operational area took in the Luftwaffe's bomber bases in the Netherlands, Belgium and France as far west as Caen in Normandy. From March 1941 onwards, the Hurricanes of No 87 Squadron joined in the Intruder missions, but it was No 23 Squadron which bore the brunt of this work throughout 1941. By the spring of that year some 80 Intruder sorties a month were being flown and 11 German aircraft fell to their guns during May.

Below:
The crew of a Boston III Intruder of No 418 Squadron RCAF prepare for take-off. This unit ended the war with 178 enemy aircraft and 79½ flying bombs destroyed to its credit, making it the top-scoring RCAF squadron. IWM CH7209

Above:
During the summer of 1941 No 247 Squadron's Hurricane IIcs began to fly Intruder operations over Brittany and a year later they added night attacks on coastal shipping to their operational repertoire.
IWM CH5486

Nearly 600 Intruder sorties were flown during 1941 for the loss of 10 RAF aircraft. In return 19 aircraft were claimed as confirmed victories or probably destroyed.

The Intruder missions flown by No 87 Squadron were concentrated over the Cherbourg peninsula and the airfields of Caen and Maupertus. Its Hurricanes, based at Charmy Down near Bath, used Warmwell in Dorset as a forward base. They generally only operated on moonlit nights, flying in pairs. One aircraft was to attack the airfield, in the hope of knocking out parked aircraft, while the

Below:
In July 1941 No 3 Squadron's Hurricane IIcs began to fly Intruder sorties from Stapleford Tawney, making use of Manston and Shoreham as forward bases. BAe

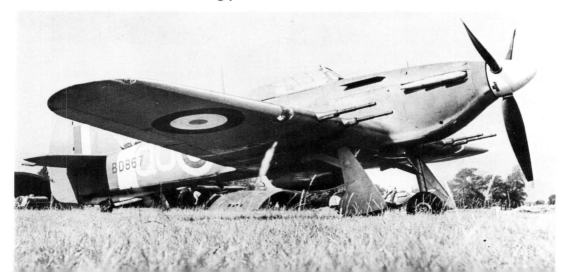

second waited above for the defences to go into action. It would then shoot up searchlights and flak emplacements. The squadron was not exclusively engaged on Intruder work at this time, as it also carried out defensive nightfighter patrols and maintained a detachment at St Mary's on the Scilly Isles. However, as the German night-bomber raids reduced in intensity after May, other Hurricane nightfighters went over to Intruder work. No 3 Squadron and No 247 Squadron began such sorties in the summer of 1941 and No 1 Squadron, destined to become the most famous of the Hurricane Intruder units, in April 1942. Because the Hurricanes were in no sense specialised nightfighter aircraft, their operations were confined to the spring and summer months. In mid-1941 the Hurricane Mk IIc, armed with four 20mm Hispano cannon, began to replace the earlier machine gun-armed variants on the nightfighter squadrons and this provided a very welcome increase in weight of fire. In the following year Intruder Hurricanes were fitted with underwing droptanks to increase their radius of action, these having been developed in 45gal and 90gal capacities. No 87 Squadron, which was still based at Charmy Down when Intruder operations over France resumed in May 1942, found the increase in range especially welcome.

A number of the Hurricane squadrons, which had trained for defensive nightfighter duties in co-operation with the largely ineffective Turbinlite Havocs, went over to Intruder duties in 1942. (They included Nos 1, 3 and 245 Squadrons.) No 1 Squadron soon emerged as the most skilful, thanks in large measure to the outstanding abilities of its

Below:
The development of jettisonable underwing fuel tanks for the Hurricane greatly increased its capabilities as an Intruder aircraft. When carrying two 44 Imp gal capacity tanks, range was extended from 425 to 900 miles; this example is fitted with a tropical filter for overseas service. BAe

CO, Sqn Ldr James Maclachlan, and the 'A' Flight commander Flt Lt Karel Kuttelwascher. Maclachlan had been seriously wounded during an air battle over Malta in February 1941 and as a result his left arm had to be amputated. He nonetheless returned to operational flying, taking command of No 1 Squadron in November 1941. Kuttelwascher had trained as a fighter pilot in his native Czechoslovakia before the German takeover in 1939. He then escaped to France and ultimately Britain, joining No 1 Squadron in October 1940. These two pilots flew the squadron's first Intruder missions on 1 April and Kuttelwascher claimed one Ju88 destroyed and a second damaged. It was an auspicious start to three months of intensive operations, during which the squadron claimed 22 enemy aircraft destroyed and 13 damaged. The greatest share of this achievement fell to Kuttelwascher, who destroyed 15 enemy aircraft and damaged a further five. Maclachlan's Intruder victories totalled five.

The night of 4/5 May was a particularly successful one for Kuttelwascher. Five Hurricanes carried out Intruder missions, one of which was flown by the CO who had shot down two German bombers on the previous night. However, he had no success that night, finding the airfields to which he was assigned shrouded in fog. Sgt J. R. Campbell attacked and destroyed a petrol tanker and two locomotives and the two other Hurricanes had inconclusive brushes with enemy aircraft and could make no claims. The Czechoslovak pilot was considerably more fortunate: he had seen no activity at Evreux, but shortly after he arrived over St André the flarepath was lit and he saw no fewer than six He111s with navigation lights burning

Below:
During his period as CO of No 1 Squadron (November 1941 to July 1942), Sqn Ldr J. A. F. Maclachlan was credited with the destruction of five enemy aircraft during Intruder missions over France. IWM CH4012

awaiting their turn to land. Kuttelwascher positioned his Hurricane Mk IIc astern and slightly below one of the bombers and on closing to 100yd he fired a 2sec burst from his cannons. His victim immediately caught fire and then dived into the ground to the northeast of the airfield; he repeated this attack on a second bomber and saw it, too, plunge down to crash. The remaining He111s seemed oblivious of the Hurricane's proximity and so Kuttelwascher was able to carry out a third attack, seeing his victim burning on the ground. Then the airfield defences woke up to the presence of a wolf in the fold: the flarepath was extinguished and AA fire criss-crossed the sky. The Czechoslovak pilot decided that it was time to leave, having gained three certain victories within the space of 15min. But as he still had about 160 rounds of ammunition remaining, Kuttelwascher flew on to the airfield at Dreux in search of further prey. However, all was quiet and so he flew back to Tangmere and landed at 02.05hrs after almost three hours in the air. Another of No 1 Squadron's pilots at this time, André Jubelin on detachment from the Free French Navy, recalled the strain of such operations for the Hurricane pilots. He wrote: 'For Intruders the struggle against fatigue began even

before they took off, during the silent watch under arms that never finished until the first light of morning. . . . The hours between twilight and dawn seemed very long.'

In March 1942 a second specialised Intruder squadron became operational. This was No 418 Squadron Royal Canadian Air Force (RCAF), which was equipped with Boston IIIs. Essentially similar to the Havoc, but with more powerful engines, the Boston III had been ordered directly from the United States, rather than taken over from French contracts. Initially it was armed in the same way as the Havoc with four nose-mounted machine guns, but this inadequate armament was later increased by fitting four 20mm cannon in a belly pack. No 23 Squadron also received Boston IIIs to supplement its Havocs. No 418 Squadron flew its first Intruder sorties on 28/29 March, when six aircraft were despatched to patrol airfields in France and the Netherlands. One crew saw a German bomber with navigation lights switched on, which was preparing to land on an illuminated flarepath. But before the Intruder could get into position to attack, it was spotted from the ground. Warning flares were fired to alert the German bomber to its danger and, as it made good its escape, the airfield lighting was switched off. Sgt G. Harding was equally unlucky on the night of 26/27 April, when he surprised a Ju88 approaching Evreux to land. He only had the opportunity for a single burst of fire — which achieved a number of hits — before the enemy

Below:
A Boston III of No 418 Squadron flies low over the coast. Note the belly gun-pack which houses four 20mm cannon. IWM CH7215

aircraft switched off its navigation lights and disappeared. Better success came on 7/8 May, when Plt Off A. Lukas carried out a bombing run on the flarepath at Gilze Rijen in the Netherlands and hit a German nightfighter just after touchdown. An intruding Hurricane from No 3 Squadron followed up the attack by strafing the enemy aircraft to complete its destruction. The hazard of Intruder operations were considerable and during its first four months of operations No 418 Squadron lost 11 aircraft and their crews. In addition to its Intruder work the squadron was sometimes required to carry out light bomber missions and leaflet-dropping. They also carried out attacks against rail targets, which towards the end of the year became more hazardous as trains began to include flak wagons for their protection. A third Intruder unit was formed in June 1942, when No 23 Squadron began to convert to the de Havilland Mosquito II and passed on its Havocs and Bostons to No 605 Squadron. The latter unit, together with No 418 Squadron RCAF, soldiered on until February 1943 when they too began to receive Mosquitos.

The start of Mosquito Intruder operations by No 23 Squadron in July 1942 marked an important milestone in the development of this combat role. In operational radius, performance and armament the Mosquito represented an immense improvement over the Bostons, Havocs and Hurricanes, which were rapidly to be phased out as the new aircraft became available to the Intruder squadrons

early in 1943. Previously, the Intruders' horizons had been limited to the arc of German airfields running from the Netherlands to western France; with the Mosquito targets as far afield as Austria and Czechoslovakia became practical propositions. Initial priority in Mosquito nightfighter deliveries had been given to the squadrons engaged on the defence of the UK and the first Intruder Mosquitos were simply conversions of the Mosquito NF Mk II stripped of its Mk IV radar and fitted with increased fuel tankage. The Mosquito FB VI which, with its internal bomb-load of 1,000lb and provision for underwing droptanks was better suited to the Intruder role, did not become available until 1943. No 23 Squadron's aircrews were generally enthusiastic about the new aircraft, their only serious misgiving being the problem of decelerating so aerodynamically-clean an aircraft should it be in danger of overshooting the target.

No 23 Squadron's first Intruder sortie on the Mosquito, appropriately flown by the CO, Wg Cdr B. R. O'Bryen Hoare on 6/7 July, was uneventful. But on the following night Hoare spotted a Dornier

Below:
Mosquito NF IIs — DZ716:L illustrated — replaced No 605 Squadron's Boston III Intruders during February 1943 and were themselves superseded by Mosquito FB VIs some six months later. The squadron claimed a total of 96 enemy aircraft destroyed on Intruder missions. IWM CH9471

Do217 flying to the east of Chartres and, after getting into a good attacking position unobserved, sent it down in flames with three bursts of cannon fire. It was the turn of Sqn Ldr K. H. Salisbury-Hughes on the night of 8/9 July — like Hoare, flying S-Sugar the only Mosquito NF Mk II then on the squadron's strength; he encountered a Do217 over Étampes and shot it down. He then went on to Evreux, where he found and attacked a He111. This aircraft exploded with such force that the Mosquito was thrown on to its back, but Salisbury-Hughes expressed himself well satisfied with his aircraft's manoeuvrability and hitting power. By the end of July, No 23 Squadron had flown 28 Mosquito sorties for the loss of only one of these aircraft and, generally, casualties continued at a low level. However, intruding remained a potentially hazardous role and during one night's operations on 8/9 September three Mosquitos failed to return. The CO himself, by then nearing the end of a gruelling tour of operations, came near to disaster on 13/14 September. He had chased after an elusive German aircraft near Twente in Holland as the weather steadily worsened. Then, as he prepared to go into the attack, the enemy pilot miscalculated and flew straight into the ground. As Hoare retreated over the coast, his starboard engine was hit by flak, so he throttled it back and feathered the propeller. The remaining engine soon afterwards began to falter and Hoare unfeathered the starboard propeller, gaining some ground before this engine finally ground to a stop. As the port engine had by then picked up somewhat, the Mosquito was able to reach the English coast. But the battery was too flat to allow the starboard propeller to be feathered again and the radio was also unusable due to loss of electrical power. With the weather steadily worsening, Hoare was nonetheless able, by a combination of good fortune and piloting skill, to bring the Mosquito in to a crash-landing at Hunsdon.

In December 1942, No 23 Squadron left Fighter Command for Malta, from whence it carried out Intruder missions against enemy transportation targets in Italy. Its departure created an interregnum in Mosquito Intruder operations, before No 418 Squadron and No 605 Squadron became operational on the type. This was partially bridged by modifying a number of the Mosquitos with the regular night defence squadrons for Intruder work. The units involved, Nos 25, 85, 151, 157 and 264 Squadrons, each had six Intruder Mosquitos. In addition to flying Intruder missions, these aircraft also undertook freelance 'Ranger' missions, both by day and night, as well as flying 'Instep' patrols over the Bay of Biscay in search of German Ju88 long range fighters and other targets. No 605 Squadron's Mosquito Intruder operations got off to a good start in February 1943, with two German bombers

destroyed over Holland. No 418 Squadron RCAF, although it received its first Mosquito on 18 February, did not retire its last Boston IIIs until September. Its first Mosquito sortie was flown by Plt Off Tony Croft on 7/8 May over the Melun-Britigny area. He sighted a Ju88 flying in the Nantes region and after a 12min chase came within range. Opening fire from 200yd range with two bursts, the Canadian pilot saw the enemy aircraft begin to burn. It then went into a slow downward spiral and was torn apart by an explosion before it reached the ground. In May, No 418 Squadron received its first Mosquito FB VI and No 605 Squadron converted on to this mark in July. During a sortie on 27/28 June, Sqn Ldr C. C. Moran of No 418 Squadron flew to Avord, where he shot down a He111 and Ju88. He also attacked a locomotive and bombed a radio mast during this sortie. Moran evolved a special method of dealing with trains, which were one of No 418 Squadron's main targets during the summer of 1943. He would open his attack by strafing with machine gun and cannon fire then, as the train came to a halt presenting a stationary target, he would run in to drop his bombs. The squadron also continued its attacks on Luftwaffe aircraft and airfields, extending its area of operations into Germany during August. By the end of September they had accounted for nine enemy aircraft destroyed, but their principal rivals, No 605 Squadron, were top-scorers during the month with 10 aircraft destroyed and two damaged to their credit.

The tremendous potential of the Mosquito for long range Intruder operations was already apparent by the end of September. No 605 Squadron had carried out sorties over Denmark and Germany, as well as over France during that month. On 15/16 September No 418 Squadron undertook a most unusual mission, providing a close escort for the Lancasters of No 617 Squadron during their attack on the Dortmund-Ems Canal. It was a mission calling for great piloting skill, for in order to maintain formation on the bombers the Mosquitos were required to fly throttled-back and with 10° of flap in order to match the Lancasters' cruising speed of 170mph. And to add to the difficulties, this had to be carried out at night and at an altitude of only 150ft. The Mosquitos successfully carried out their assigned task of protecting the bombers from nightfighters en route to the target and they attempted to deal with the canal's flak and searchlight defences as the Lancasters bombed. However, in this they were less successful. Losses to the German defences were heavy and five out of the eight Lancasters despatched on this mission failed to return. At the end of September the redoubtable Wg Cdr Hoare returned to combat duty as CO of No 605 Squadron, having set up a specialised Intruder training squadron within No 51

OTU at Cranfield during his rest from operations. On his first sortie after taking over the squadron on 27/28 September, Hoare shot down a Do217 over Dedelsdorf. It was his seventh confirmed night victory and he was also credited with four enemy aircraft probably destroyed and four damaged at that time.

From January 1944 until the D-Day landings in June, the Intruder squadrons concentrated their efforts against German airfields and aircraft. On 10/11 January, Hoare shot down a Ju188 in the vicinity of Chièvres for his squadron's 100th victory. On 27 January the rival No 418 Squadron RCAF took advantage of low cloud cover over France to carry out 'Day Ranger' missions. Four Mosquitos, operating in pairs, claimed a record bag of seven enemy aircraft destroyed, but this was bettered on 3 May when 11 aircraft were destroyed and four damaged in a 'Ranger' mission over Germany. The successful pilots were Flg Off C. C. Scherf and Flt Lt J. T. Caine. No 605 Squadron, whose activities were confined to night Intruder missions, did not have the same opportunities for scoring, but nonetheless performed well, claiming 17 victories in March for the loss of only one Mosquito. On 5/6 June as the Normandy invasion got underway No 605 Squadron flew 18 sorties in support, attacking ground targets in the Caen area. And that night the first enemy aircraft to be shot down during the landings, an Me410, fell to the guns of a No 605 Squadron Mosquito piloted by Flg Off R. E. Lelong.

The two Intruder squadrons were then diverted for a time to anti-'Diver' sorties, to intercept V-1 Flying Bombs. However, when Intruder operations resumed, the Mosquitos then had the great advantage of the use of advanced bases in France and consequently were able to extend their operations to such remote areas of Reich territory as Czechoslovakia, East Prussia and Austria. By mid-November 1944 with the advance of the Allied armies to the borders of the Rhine, Intruder operations as such came to an end and No 418 Squadron RCAF and No 605 Squadron were transferred to the 2nd Tactical Air Force as fighter-bomber units.

The work of the Intruders had for a long time been of general assistance to RAF Bomber Command, as they greatly increased the danger of night operations for the *Nachtjagdgruppen* by their forays over German airfields. However, with the implementation of Operation 'Flower' in June 1943 this support became much more directly integrated with the RAF's bomber operations. It was arranged that Intruders should carry out patrols over the German nightfighter bases during the times when

Below:
No 29 Squadron operated Mosquito NF XIIIs on Intruder missions over France, the Low Countries and Germany from May 1944 until February 1945. HK382:T is seen at its Hunsdon dispersal in January 1945. IWM CH14643

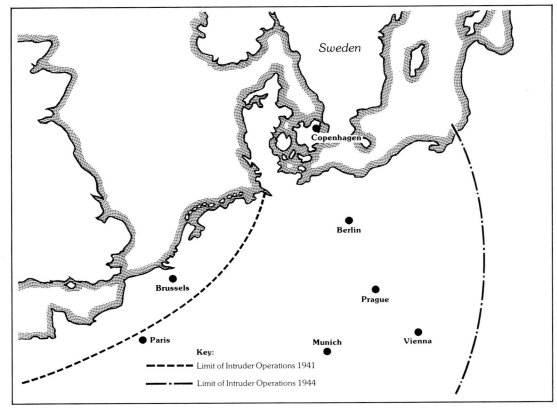

 — note: map contains the following labels:

Sweden

Copenhagen

Berlin

Brussels

Prague

Paris

Munich   Vienna

Key:
– – – – – Limit of Intruder Operations 1941
– · – · – Limit of Intruder Operations 1944

RAF Intruder Operations

Bomber Command would be penetrating enemy airspace. Initially each known nightfighter airfield was allocated to a Mosquito crew. This duty was carried out by the Intruder aircraft attached to RAF Fighter Command's defensive nightfighter squadrons, as well as to Nos 418 and 605 Squadrons. By late 1943 the 'Flower' sorties had been elaborated, so that an initial attack on the nightfighter bases went in just before the RAF bomber stream's approach and then a second force of patrolling Mosquitos attempted to harry the nightfighters as they returned to land at the end of their sorties. In May 1944 it was decided to allow AI-equipped Mosquitos to fly on Intruder operations and No 29 Squadron flew the first of these sorties on 14/15 May.

The activities of No 29 Squadron (based at Hunsdon) on the night of 18/19 September 1944 give a good idea of the character of Operation 'Flower' patrols. That night Bomber Command despatched 213 aircraft to attack Bremerhaven. The first of three Mosquito NF XIIIs fitted with AI Mk VIII took off at 20.10hrs to patrol Gütersloh and Paderborn. While en route to the patrol area the Mosquito was coned by searchlights, but these were easily shaken off in a dive. Two airfields were seen with their flarepaths lit, but when the Mosquito — flown by Flg Off Butterworth — reached its assigned patrol area, both airfields were inactive. Butterworth therefore flew back to the area where he had seen lighting, but by that time they too were quiet. He returned to base, landing at 23.55hrs. Flg Off Slater's Mosquito was airborne at 20.25hrs bound for Stade and Nordholz. On arriving he found both airfields' beacons flashing, but no aircraft were seen. After leaving the patrol area, he saw recognition flares fired from an aircraft in the Quakenbruck area, but on turning towards this activity, no contact could be picked up on radar. With fuel running low, the Mosquito landed at Coltishall at 00.48hrs. The third Intruder took off for Leeuwarden in Holland at 20.55hrs. When over that airfield an aircraft was seen eight miles away under fire from flak. It immediately fired recognition flares and the shooting stopped. However, by the time the Mosquito had turned towards the aircraft and closed the distance, no radar contact could be made. The Mosquito returned to base and landed at 00.10hrs. The lack of any positive results from this night's activity was perhaps more typical of the routine of Intruder operations than the nights of dramatic success. Yet, such patrolling did maintain pressure on the Luftwaffe's nightfighters and, even when the Intruder carried AI radar, contact with enemy aircraft was still very much a matter of chance.

Another means of assisting Bomber Command's operations was by hunting down the German nightfighters in the air, before they could reach the bomber stream. Known as Bomber Support missions, these tactics were pioneered by the Beaufighters of No 141 Squadron during the summer of 1943. The squadron, based at Wittering under the command of Wg Cdr J. R. D. Braham, was placed directly under Headquarters Fighter Command for the Bomber Support operational trials, bypassing the usual intermediate sector station and group levels of command. Bomber Command would pass information on the coming night's operations to Intruder Control at HQ Fighter Command and the latter would pass this on to the squadron. Its Beaufighters were specially equipped with 'Serrate', a device for homing on to German airborne radar emissions, and AI Mk IV. Serrate could provide an accurate bearing on the target and indicate its elevation relative to the intercepting aircraft, but AI was needed to provide range information. As Serrate had a range of about 100 miles, it was used to obtain the initial contact. The Beaufighter's RO would then complete the interception using his AI radar when the range had closed. Rather than attempting to provide a close escort to the bomber stream, which would have been difficult to accomplish satisfactorily at night, Braham aimed to interpose his Beaufighters between it and the Luftwaffe nightfighter bases.

No 141 Squadron began operations with Serrate on the night of 14/15 June 1943, when Bomber Command carried out a raid on Oberhausen. Six Beaufighters were despatched using Coltishall in Norfolk as a forward base. The CO himself, flying with Flt Lt W. J. Gregory, was the only pilot to have any success. He had patrolled the Deelen area for over an hour and was returning to the coast when Gregory picked up a German nightfighter closing in on the Beaufighter from astern. Braham turned hard to port to get on to its tail, but as he did so the enemy aircraft also turned in the same direction. However, Braham outmanoeuvred it and gained a firing position on his opponent, which he identified as a Messerschmitt Bf110, at 400yd range off the port beam. After firing an opening burst of 5sec with cannon and machine gun, Braham throttled-back and prepared to resume the attack. But his first burst was sufficient — it had raked the enemy aircraft's fuselage from tail to cockpit and set its port engine on fire. The Bf110 went into a vertical dive and crashed in flames. After almost three hours in the air, the Beaufighter was low on fuel and so Braham

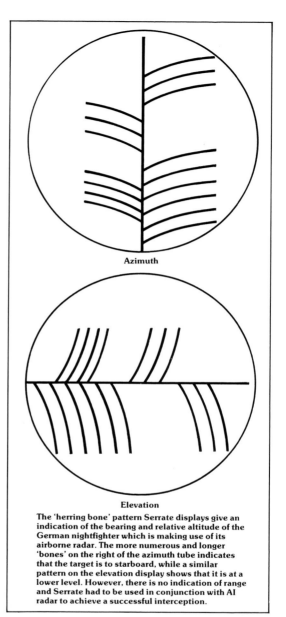

Azimuth

Elevation

The 'herring bone' pattern Serrate displays give an indication of the bearing and relative altitude of the German nightfighter which is making use of its airborne radar. The more numerous and longer 'bones' on the right of the azimuth tube indicates that the target is to starboard, while a similar pattern on the elevation display shows that it is at a lower level. However, there is no indication of range and Serrate had to be used in conjunction with AI radar to achieve a successful interception.

Serrate Displays

headed back to base. Two nights later he succeeded in damaging a Ju88 and on 24/25 June shot down a second Bf110. Yet, notwithstanding these victories, it was apparent to Braham that the Beaufighter lacked sufficient range to perform effectively in the Bomber Support role. When the bombers' targets were distant objectives like Berlin or northern Italy, Braham was forced to split his squadron's effort, sending out half of the Beaufighters to cover their outward flight for as long as

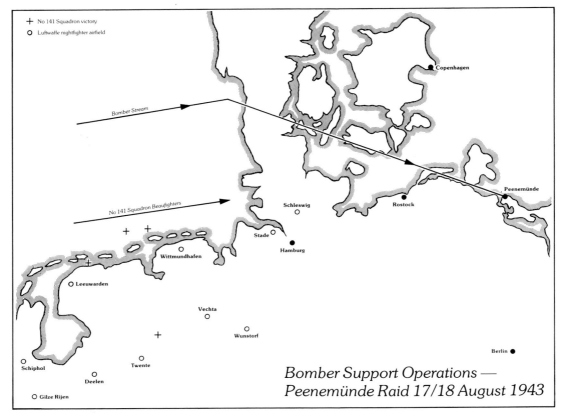

Key:
+ No 141 Squadron victory
○ Luftwaffe nightfighter airfield

Copenhagen

Bomber Stream

Peenemünde

No 141 Squadron Beaufighters

Schleswig ○

Rostock ●

+ +

Stade ●

+ Hamburg ●

○ Wittmundhafen

○ Leeuwarden

Vechta ○

+ Wunstorf ○

Berlin ●

○ Schiphol

Twente ○

○ Deelen

○ Gilze Rijen

Bomber Support Operations —
Peenemünde Raid 17/18 August 1943

the aircraft's endurance permitted and reserving the rest to meet the returning bombers.

Despite these handicaps, No 141 Squadron's Beaufighters convincingly demonstrated the potential of the Bomber Support role. On the night of 17/18 August, when Bomber Command raided the rocket research establishment at Peenemünde, the squadron took on the Bf110s of *IV Gruppe Nachtjagdgeschwader 1*, under the formidable Lt Heinz-Wolfgang Schnaufer, and emerged the clear victors. Two of the German nightfighters were shot down by Braham and the Beaufighters escaped without loss. On 29/30 September Braham scored another noteworthy victory, shoot-

Left:
Wg Cdr J. R. D. Braham (right) — pictured with his regular navigator Flt Lt W. J. Gregory — pioneered the Bomber Support mission in 1943 when commanding No 141 Squadron. IWM CH13176

ing down the Bf110 flown by 53-victory ace Hauptmann August Geiger of *NJG 1*, over the Zuider Zee. Ten minutes later he encountered a Ju88, which he succeeded in damaging before he was denied a second definite victory when his guns failed. It was Braham's last operation before his tour in command of No 141 Squadron finished; it also marked the end of No 141 Squadron's use of the Beaufighter. The unit then began to convert to the Mosquito, which was much better suited to the Bomber Support role. The first Mosquitos to be used for Bomber Support were aircraft of the Fighter Interception Unit at Ford, which began operations in August 1943. The FIU conducted trials with tail-warning radar, codenamed 'Monica', which was in fact a modified AI Mk IV set. Using this equipment, the Mosquito would allow a German nightfighter to approach to within about 5,000ft astern. It would then pull around in a tight turn to get behind the enemy aircraft. As the German *Lichtenstein* airborne radar had a narrow beam, which gave coverage only for about 25° either side of the centreline, it was hoped that the German nightfighter crew would be confused by the Mosquito's manoeuvre and take no evasive action. Continuing its well established tradition of carrying out actual operations during its trials programmes, the FIU flew many Bomber Support operations during 1943-44. However, as the unit had few Mosquitos these operations were perforce on a small scale. The Mosquito Intruders of No 605 Squadron also carried out similar missions at this time, but unlike FIU's aircraft they carried no radar.

In November 1943 Bomber Support Operations came under the control of the newly-formed No 100 Group of Bomber Command, which was responsible not only for the offensive nightfighter patrols but also for Radio Countermeasures. In addition to No 141 Squadron, which began operations with Serrate-equipped Mosquitos on 3 November, two new Mosquito squadrons were assigned to No 100 Group. They were Nos 169 and 239 Squadrons, which had both previously flown Mustangs on fighter-reconnaissance duties. (A fourth unit, No 515 Squadron, flew Mosquito FB VI Intruders.) The inexperience of these new units combined with the unsuitability of much of their equipment, resulted in relatively poor results from the first three months of operations. The Mosquito II aircraft with which the squadrons were equipped were elderly airframes in need of refurbishment; their AI Mk IV radar was obsolescent and when working near the bomber stream it was difficult to marry up returns from Serrate with numerous contacts on the radar. Between December 1943 and April 1944, 220 sorties were completed by these squadrons, which claimed 27 enemy aircraft destroyed and four damaged. And to add to the already considerable problems of interception, the effectiveness of the Serrate equipment steadily declined during this period. This was because the *Lichtenstein* radar on to which it homed was rapidly being phased out of service in favour of the improved *SN-2* set. The RAF had yet to identify this

RAF Bomber Support Operations 1943-45					
Month	No of Sorties	RAF Losses	Claims		
			Destroyed	Probable	Damaged
December 1943	11	1	1	0	1
January 1944	41	1	4	0	0
February 1944	89	3	4	0	2
March 1944	135	4	6	0	2
April 1944	241	7	15	1	0
May 1944	332	8	18	0	1
June 1944	650	4	28	1	5
July 1944	650	4	25	0	5
August 1944	553	2	7	0	6
September 1944	708	9	33	2	17
October 1944	719	5	12	2	8
November 1944	689	4	14	3	9
December 1944	624	2	38	1	7
January 1945	426	3	18	0	3
February 1945	674	3	10	1	5
March 1945	644	6	16	1	5
April 1945	698	3	15	2	4

new radar and so Serrate had not been modified to pick up its emissions.

Bomber Command's disastrous losses during the Nuremberg Raid of 30/31 March 1944 (95 aircraft out of 782 despatched) forced a thorough-going reappraisal of Bomber Support policy. Air Chief Marshal Sir Arthur Harris demanded that a minimum of 10 Mosquito squadrons be made available for nightfighter escort duties and he pressed that the much-improved centimetric radars, AI Mk VIII and Mk X, be released for use over enemy territory. In the event only three additional squadrons were transferred to No 100 Group (Nos 23, 85 and 157 Squadrons). The latter two units flew centimetric radar-equipped nightfighters, while No 23 Squadron's Mosquito FB VIs joined No 515 Squadron on Intruder work. Even this modest increase of strength was welcome and, in combination with improved equipment and growing operational experience, it began to produce better results. On the night of 20/21 July 1944 the Group's 100th nightfighter victory was gained by No 169 Squadron's CO, Wg Cdr N. B. R. Bromley. A week earlier, on the night of 12/13 July, the RAF had acquired an example of the *SN-2* radar, when a Ju88 night-fighter landed in error at Woodbridge in Suffolk. This windfall enabled a modified version on Serrate to be produced, which covered the radar's operating frequency. Another useful homing device, codenamed 'Perfectos', became available to the RAF nightfighters in November 1944. This worked by triggering the German nightfighters' FuG 25a IFF (Identification, Friend or Foe) equipment, thus providing the RAF nightfighter with an accurate range and bearing on its target, as well as positive proof that it was an enemy aircraft. Once Perfectos was known to the Germans, though, it was countered quite simply by switching off the IFF sets. In the latter part of 1944 the Mosquito FB VIs were fitted with centimetric radar (the American ASH equipment, known to the RAF as AI Mk XV, which was packaged into a compact cylinder easily fitted into the Mosquito's nose).

Thus by late 1944 the Bomber Support squadron's nightfighters were well equipped for their long range missions, typically carrying a centimetric AI, Monica tail-warning radar, Perfectos or Serrate and the Gee long range navigation aid. Some progress had also been made towards solving the perennial problem of distinguishing friendly from enemy nightfighters by the fitting of infra-red identification equipment. The tactics of the Bomber Support fighters had likewise been expanded and refined. As early attempts to bring the German nightfighters to combat over their known assembly points had largely failed, a three-phase plan of operations was devised to bring the Bomber Support Mosquitos into contact with them. Initially, patrols were despatched to the German nightfighter airfields, which were timed to arrive just before the bomber force showed up on the enemy early-warning radars. Armed with bombs in addition to their cannon, these aircraft would attempt to prevent the defenders from getting airborne. A second force of Bomber Support nightfighters would establish a screen between the German aircraft and RAF bombers. Patrolling about 40 miles from their charges, they therefore had some 8min after contacting an enemy fighter to bring it down or otherwise prevent it getting into the bomber stream. Lastly, another group of Bomber Support fighters was sent over the German airfields in the hope of catching the defenders on their return.

Total claims by No 100 Group's nightfighters for the period December 1943 to April 1945 amounted to 257 enemy aircraft destroyed, of which 21 had been caught on the ground. During the same period only 69 Mosquitos were lost. In spite of the great complexity of these operations and the modest forces engaged (which never reached Harris's minimum requirement of 10 squadrons), good results had been obtained. Had the nightfighter forces of No 100 Group been substantially strengthened, they could have played a major role in the defeat of the Luftwaffe's *Nachtjagdgruppen*. As it was, their impact on the morale of the Luftwaffe's nightfighter pilots was considerable. Air Cdre Roderick Chisholm, Senior Air Staff Officer at No 100 Group Headquarters and himself a notable nightfighter pilot, reported of the postwar interrogation of German nightfighter crews, 'it was satisfying to find a generally accepted belief in the dominance of the Mosquito fighters'.

For the Luftwaffe, Intruder operations were one of the great missed opportunities of the war. During 1940-41 a single *Gruppe*, I/NJG 2, had operated in this role over Britain. However, their activities had then been discontinued by direct orders of the Führer, leaving Bomber Command free to operate over its own airfields virtually without hindrance. A few scattered raids by German bomber aircraft against these bases had little impact, but some idea of the effects of a sustained Intruder campaign can be gained from the results of a brief resurgence of German Intruder activity in March 1945. These sorties, codenamed Operation 'Gisela', were believed to be the brainchild of Maj Schnaufer (the Kommodore of NJG 4). Similar in conception to the German dayfighters' Operation 'Bodenplatte' on New Year's Day 1945, this onslaught took the British by surprise, but came too late to achieve any lasting results. On 3/4 March over 100 German Ju88 nightfighters followed the RAF bomber stream back to Britain, where 22 four-engined bombers fell to their guns. Three further Intruder missions followed, but they were on a much smaller scale. Thus German efforts amounted to little more than a postscript to the history of Intruder operations.

4 The Luftwaffe's Nightfighter Force

Germany's experience of nightfighter operations during World War 1 had not been as extensive as Britain's, nor had specialised squadrons and command and control systems been formed for this role. Consequently, night-fighting was neglected during the Luftwaffe's build-up in the 1930s and by the outbreak of World War 2 only a small number of Messerschmitt Bf109 *Staffeln* were assigned to the mission. Their operations were, perforce, confined to clear nights and they, like their RAF 'Cat's Eyes' counterparts, relied on searchlights for target illumination. The German neglect of the nightfighter was primarily due to the confidence placed in the Flak regiments for night air defence. Well equipped and highly trained, the AA artillery and searchlight troops, which formed part of the Luftwaffe, were something of an élite force. However, practical experience was soon to show that the effectiveness of the Flak arm against nightbombers had been greatly overestimated. In May 1940 the RAF began bombing attacks on Germany, having previously restricted its bombers to leaflet raids. It then became apparent that the Luftwaffe would have to build up a specialised nightfighter force to counter this

threat. But, because of this late start, it was not to be until the end of 1942 that Germany possessed a nightfighter arm which was able to threaten the RAF raiders.

The officer made responsible for forming and leading the first nightfighter *Geschwader* was Hpt Wolfgang Falk, the *Kommandeur* of *I Gruppe Zerstörergeschwader 1*. His *Gruppe*, equipped with the Messerschmitt Bf110, was to form the nucleus of *Nachtjagdgeschwader 1* as *I/NJG 1*. In June 1940 it was sent to Düsseldorf, from where it began experimental night sorties in defence of the Ruhr. Meanwhile, a second *Gruppe* of nightfighters, *II/NJG 1*, began training on the Junkers Ju88C, while the existing Bf109 nightfighter *Staffeln* became *III/NJG 1*. Falk, as the *Geschwaderkommo-*

Below:
Bf 110C nightfighters of *III/NJG 4*. First formed in the spring of 1942, this *Gruppe* was low on the priority list for delivery of *Lichtenstein B/C* airborne radar. The further aircraft is that of Oberfeldwebel Reinhard Kollack, who ended the war with 49 victories to his credit. Bundesarchiv

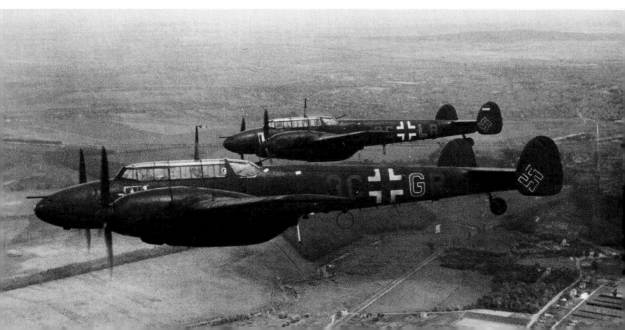

Above:
The Luftwaffe's early plans for a nightfighter force emphasised the long range offensive mission; *II Gruppe* **of** *NJG 1* **(later redesignated** *I/NJG 2)* **was intended to form the nucleus of an Intruder force of three** *Geschwader.* **A key aircraft in this programme was the Junkers Ju88 C-series of long range fighters; a Jumo 211J-powered C-6 is illustrated.**
Bundesarchiv

Right:
Oblt Werner Streib was one of the founder members of the Luftwaffe's nightfighter force and in July 1943 he became Kommodore of *Nachtjagdgeschwader 1.* **He ended the war with 66 victories to his credit, all but one of which were gained at night.** Bundesarchiv 78/106/21

dore of *NJG 1*, had to weld this heterogeneous assembly into an effective fighting force, evolving suitable night-fighting tactics and command and control procedures as he went along. Fortunately he was an officer possessed of great energy and organising ability. A system of ground-controlled night-fighting, operating in conjunction with searchlights was quickly worked out. As the nightfighter force expanded, Falk was relegated to a subordinate position, but his pioneering work was suitably commemorated in the crest carried by the *Nachtjagdgruppen* fighters throughout the war. It depicted a diving falcon, 'Falk' being the German for falcon.

On 19/20 July, Oblt Werner Streib gained *I/NJG 1's* first night victory over the Rühr. It was a

Above:
The Dornier Do17Z-6 *Kauz 1* (Screech Owl) was adapted from the Do17Z-3 bomber specifically for the long range Intruder role. It carried a crew of three and additional fuel tanks in the forward bomb bay. Dornier DWN98/86400

clear night when he began his patrol shortly after midnight, taking off from Gutersloh where a detachment had moved to escape from the industrial haze of the Ruhr. After nearly two hours of fruitless searching, Streib picked up another aircraft flying 300yd ahead of his Bf110 and slightly below it. He closed in to short range and identified it as a Whitley. Streib then broke away to make a second approach for his attack. As the Bf110 got to within 250yd of the RAF bomber, it was seen by the rear gunner who opened fire. Streib took careful aim and fired two short bursts of cannon and machine gun fire into the Whitley. Its starboard engine caught fire and Streib reported that two of its crew baled out. However, the RAF bomber continued flying, although it turned away from its target and headed back to friendly territory. Streib carried out a further attack, again firing two bursts into the bomber and, as he met no more return fire, closed in to short range. The RAF bomber turned on to its back and dived into the ground. Streib was to become one of the most successful of the early German nightfighter aces, ending the war with 66 victories to his credit (one of which was gained by day). In October 1940 he became *Kommandeur* of I/NJG 1 and he succeeded Falk as *Geschwader-*

kommodore in July 1943. In 1944 he became Inspector of Nightfighters on the Staff of Gen Adolf Galland. Streib's successes were quickly followed by others and by the end of 1940 the nightfighters had 42 victories to their credit.

On 17 July the Luftwaffe formed a nightfighter division, under the command of Ob Josef Kammhuber, to co-ordinate and control the efforts of the rapidly growing *Nachtjagdgruppen*. The 44-year-old Kammhuber had served as an infantryman during World War 1 and remained in the small peacetime army, before transferring to the Luftwaffe in 1933. After holding various staff appointments, he had taken command of KG 51 and fought with the unit during the French campaign. Despite his undoubted efficiency and competence, he lacked ability as leader and was generally disliked by subordinates. By the end of 1940 the three *Gruppen* of NJG 1 had been reinforced by I and II *Gruppe* of NJG 2 and I *Gruppe* of NJG 3. This expansion was made possible by transferring a number of the *Zerstörer* units to night-fighting duties and by detaching *Staffeln* from NJG 1 to form the nucleus of a new *Gruppe*. The single-seat Bf109 had disappeared from the *Nachtjagdgruppen* inventory by the end of 1940, its 195 aircraft strength by then mainly comprising Bf110s. Junkers Ju88Cs equipped one *Gruppe* and small numbers of Dornier Do17Z *Kauz II* nightfighters were also in service. The reliance on the Bf110 was to cause Kammhuber considerable problems during 1941-42, because production of this type was run down during the period in anticipation of its

replacement by the Me210. However, the new aircraft was a failure and so the Bf110 had to be put back into production to fill the gap. As a result, the nightfighter force suffered serious aircraft shortages before Bf110 deliveries regained their momentum in mid-1942. Nonetheless, by August 1941 the force and its supporting ground organisation had grown to a sufficient extent to justify the creation of *Fliegerkorps XII* to control it. Kammhuber, pro-

Above:
The pilot's instrument panel of a Do17Z nightfighter. Note the *Revi* gunsight mounted on the cockpit coaming. Dornier DWF3092/18

moted to Generalleutnant, remained in overall command.

In October 1940 Kammhuber was able to introduce limited radar-directed ground control for

Right:
Armament of the Do17Z-6 comprised three 7.9mm MG 17 machine guns and a 20mm Oerlikon MG FF cannon mounted beneath the machine guns. The latter weapon was drum-fed, it being the flight engineer's responsibility to reload it when necessary.
Dornier DWN98/86399

Left:
General der Flieger Josef Kammhuber was the architect of the Luftwaffe's nightfighter force. Appointed to command the Night-Fighter Division in July 1940, he remained in command of all nightfighter units until his dismissal in September 1943. Bundesarchiv

nated night-fighting), the system had many disadvantages. Even a moderate degree of cloud cover reduced its efficiency. The range of the early *Würzburg A* radars was only some 18 miles, although the *Würzburg-Riese* which became available in 1941 extended this to about 50 miles. Only one nightfighter at the time could be controlled by a zone and, because the Germans did not then have IFF (Identification, Friend or Foe) equipment, the nightfighter and its target could easily be confused. But for all its drawbacks, the system did improve the nightfighters' chances of interception. The first radar-directed victory was recorded by Lt Ludwig Becker of II/NJG 1 flying a Do17Z *Kauz II*, on the night of 2 October 1940. By 1941 the radar-directed illuminated night-fighting zones had been extended to cover a coastal belt stretching from Belgium up to the Danish frontier.

Kammhuber however realised that illuminated night-fighting was not a fully satisfactory answer to the problems of night defence. He therefore evolved a radar-directed system which eliminated the need for searchlight illumination. Known by the codename *Himmelbett* (four-poster bed), it com-

the nightfighters. Six *Würzburg* radars, which had been produced for the Flak units, were allocated to the nightfighter division. Three nightfighter zones were then established, each manned by a searchlight battalion and two radar companies. One of the radars was responsible for directing and tracking the nightfighter, while a second worked with the searchlights which had the job of target illumination. Known as *Helle Nachtjagd* (illumi-

Below:
A pair of Bf110G nightfighters of *NJG 6* equipped with *Lichtenstein B/C* radar. This unit was formed in August 1943 and was based in Southern Germany. Bundesarchiv 659/6436/15

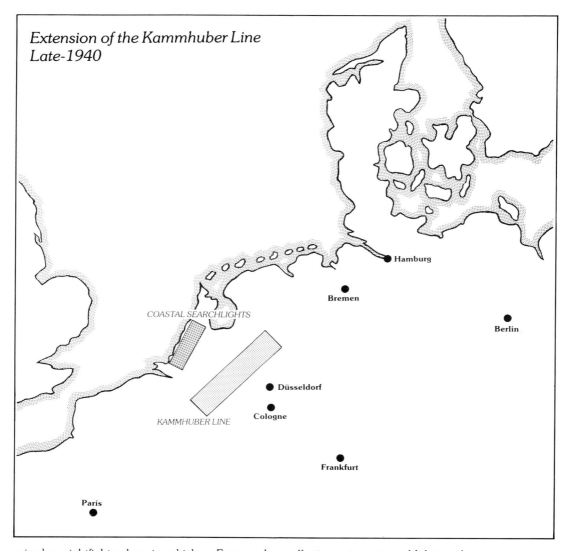

Extension of the Kammhuber Line
Late-1940

COASTAL SEARCHLIGHTS

KAMMHUBER LINE

Hamburg

Bremen

Berlin

Düsseldorf

Cologne

Frankfurt

Paris

prised a nightfighter box in which a *Freya* radar provided area surveillance, while two *Würzburg* radars carried out target tracking and fighter direction. Such was the accuracy attainable in plotting the position of target and nightfighter, that the ground controller was able to bring the latter within visual range of its quarry. An interlocking series of *Himmelbett* boxes was positioned to form a barrier along the RAF nightbombers' approaches to the Ruhr. By the spring of 1941 it had been extended northeastwards to reach the Danish frontier and, with the availability of the *Würzburg-Riese* radar, its depth of coverage was increased. The RAF paid the system's instigator the compliment of christening it the Kammhuber Line.

So long as the nightfighters were only required to operate on clear nights, the *Himmelbett* system was effective, since it could bring the interceptor to within about 400yd of its quarry. However, it was realised from the first that an airborne detection device for the nightfighters was highly desirable. An infra-red detection system, known as *Spanner*, was experimented with in the summer of 1940, but it was found to lack the necessary range. Kammhuber had called for the development of airborne radar and by the middle of 1941 the Telefunken company's *Lichtenstein B/C* had reached a sufficiently advanced state of development to justify production. With a minimum range of some 200yd, it enabled the nightfighters to operate effectively in conditions of poor visibility. The first experimental *Lichtenstein* sets reached *NJG 1* in the summer of 1941, but they were initially regarded with distrust by the more experienced nightfighter crews. The

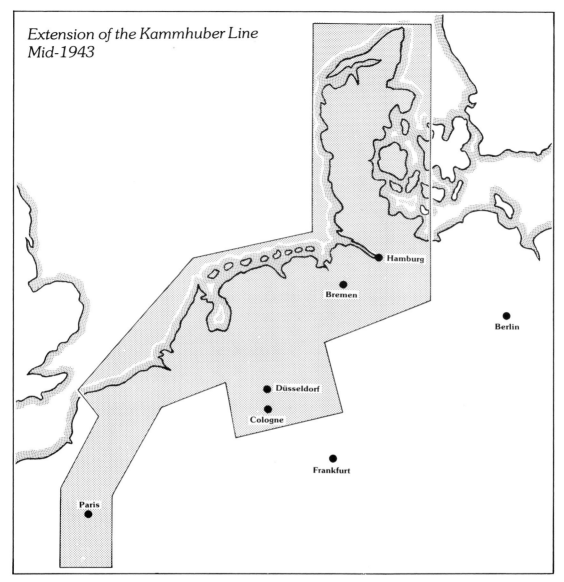

Extension of the Kammhuber Line Mid-1943

Hamburg

Bremen

Berlin

Düsseldorf

Cologne

Frankfurt

Paris

equipment's high-drag aerial array knocked some 25mph off the Bf110's speed and the crews who had gained good results by visual target acquisition could see no need for the new equipment. Their attitude was changed by Oberleutnant Ludwig Becker of *II/NJG 1*, who gained the first *Lichtenstein* victory on 10 August 1941. Significantly, he was flying a Do215B, a much larger and heavier nightfighter than the Bf110. By the end of September he had shot down a further five RAF bombers. Yet, as the first production *Lichtenstein* radars did not reach the *Nachtjagdgruppen* until early 1942, his achievements were as yet an isolated omen of future success.

Yet, in spite of all the efforts to create an effective nightfighter force, it appeared by late 1941 as though the RAF bombers were more than holding their own in the contest. Only 52 victories had been claimed by the nightfighters between October and December and even an improvement in their performance in 1942 only resulted in an attrition rate of some 4% of RAF Bomber Command sorties. On the night of 30/31 May 1942, when the RAF despatched its first 1,000-bomber raid to Cologne, the combined efforts of flak and nightfighters accounted for 37 of the raiders. However, a steady improvement in the nightfighters' organisation and standard of equipment was maintained. *Flieger-*

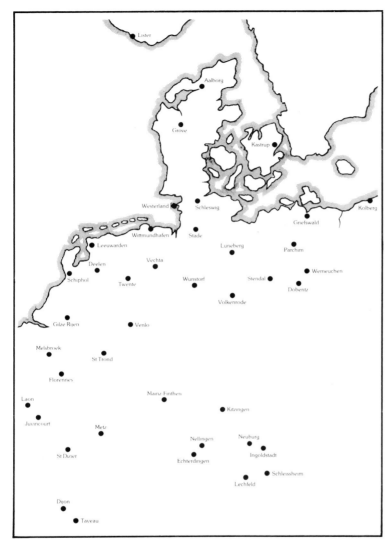

Principal Luftwaffe Nightfighter Bases

korps XII was reorganised in May to create three subordinate fighter divisions, in place of the single nightfighter division. A new nightfighter, the Do217J, entered service in March 1942, but its performance proved to be unsatisfactory. Re-equipment of the nightfighter force with production-standard *Lichtenstein* radars began in February, but it was not until 1943 that the equipment was in widespread service. The deepening and extension of the Kammhuber Line continued, so that by the end of the year it stretched from south of Paris to the northern tip of Jutland and covered many of the industrial areas behind the main barrier. Certain shortcomings remained: it was

still possible for the RAF's bombers to circumvent the defences, although to do so required extensive detours. More seriously, the system was liable to become quickly saturated, since only one nightfighter could be controlled by each box. Nevertheless, the cumulative process of expansion and improvement of the German night defences resulted in a formidably effective system by the end of 1942.

Aircraft supply problems had at last been overcome, permitting an appreciable increase of the nightfighter force from a strength of 15 *Gruppen* at the end of 1942 up to 22 *Gruppen* by mid-1943. In response to mounting losses, RAF Bomber

Luftwaffe Nightfighter Force July 1943

Unit	CO/Base	Aircraft
NJG 1	**Oberst W. Streib**	
Stab	Deelen	Bf110
I Gruppe	Venlo	Bf110
II Gruppe	St Trond	Bf110
III Gruppe	Twente	Bf110
IV Gruppe	Leeuwarden	Bf110
NJG 2	**Oberstleutnant K. Hülshoff**	
Non-operational	Reforming in Netherlands	
NJG 3	**Oberst H. Lent**	
Stab	Stade	Bf110
I Gruppe	Vechta, Wittmundhafen	Do217, Ju88, Bf110
II Gruppe	Schleswig	Do217, Ju88, Bf110
	Westerland	
III Gruppe	Lüneberg	Bf110
	Wunstorf	
	Stade	
IV Gruppe	Grove	Do217, Ju88
	Kastrup	
Nachtjagd-Kommando 190	Aalborg	Fw190
NJG 4	**Oberstleutnant Stoltenhoff**	
Stab	Metz	Do217, Bf110
I Gruppe	Florennes	Do217, Bf110
II Gruppe	St Dizier	Do217, Bf110
III Gruppe	Juvincourt	Do217, Bf110
IV Gruppe	Mainz-Finthen	Bf110
NJG 5	**Oberstleutnant Schaffer**	
Stab	Döberitz	Bf110
I Gruppe	Stendal	Bf110
	Volkenrode	
II Gruppe	Parchim	Bf110
	Greifswald	
III Gruppe	Werneuchen	Bf110
	Kolberg	
	Greifswald	
JG 300	**Oberst H-J Herrmann**	
Stab	Bonn-Hangelar	Bf109, Fw190
I Gruppe	Bonn-Hangelar	Bf109, Fw190
II Gruppe	Rheine	Fw190
III Gruppe	Oldenburg	Bf109

Command modified its tactics in the spring of 1943 to achieve a greater concentration over the target. A bomber stream, led by target-marking pathfinders, would complete its attack within a period of about 30min. This force penetrated the Kammhuber Line defences much more quickly than hitherto and as a consequence the controlled nightfighters' chances of interception were greatly reduced. The Germans countered these tactics by further deepening the Kammhuber Line defences and by increasing the control capacity of each box so that two or more nightfighters could be handled at once. During the Battle of the Ruhr, between March and June 1943, the night defences brought down a total of 572 RAF bombers. However, this represented an attrition rate of only 4.7%, whereas a rate of at least 10% was needed if Bomber Command was to be defeated. Kammhuber put forward an ambitious expansion plan, which would more than quadruple the nightfighters' strength. Not surprisingly, this was thrown out by the German High Command.

The Bf110 and Ju88 remained the mainstay of the nightfighter force throughout 1942-43, the Bf110F-4 and Ju88C-6 variants being the most widely used. Both were considered too slow, although the Ju88C-6 was otherwise a well-liked aircraft. A new and more powerful version of the Messerschmitt nightfighter, the Bf110G-4, entered service in April 1943, but its development had been rushed and as a result numerous teething problems were experienced. A specialised nightfighter — the Heinkel He219 — was under test, but Kammhuber was unable to obtain the necessary priority to accelerate its introduction into service. Maj Werner Streib carried out operational trials of the new fighter on the night of 11/12 June 1943, during a Bomber Command raid on Düsseldorf. In the course of this single sortie he shot down no fewer than five RAF bombers. It was a convincing demonstration of the He219's capabilities, although somewhat marred by the nightfighter crashing on its return to base (fortunately without injury to Streib or his radar operator). But, in spite of its great promise, deliveries of the He219 were sluggish and a year after its successful combat debut only about 30 of these aircraft were in operational service.

The Bf110 was by a considerable margin the most numerous of the German nightfighters in mid-1943 and it was not until the later months of 1944 that it was to be superseded. A typical Bf110 combat sortie of this period was flown on the night of 21/22 June 1943 by Lt Heinz-Wolfgang Schnaufer of II/NJG 1. He was ordered off from St Trond in Belgium at 00.54hrs and 25min later was directed to intercept a lone aircraft, which had become detached from the main bomber stream. His radar operator picked up the target at 2,500yd range and, in closing in to 500yd, Schnaufer recognised it as a Short Stirling. The RAF bomber carried out violent evasive manoeuvres, but Schnaufer nonetheless fired an accurate burst into its wings and fuselage. The Stirling caught fire and dived into the ground. It was Schnaufer's 13th victory, his first having been gained a year earlier. But this slow start was deceptive: in March 1944 he shot down his 50th bomber and in late October he became only the second pilot to score 100 victories by night. Schnaufer's final score of 121 night victories was unsurpassed by any other airman.

The limitations of the *Himmelbett* system led certain Luftwaffe officers to question the validity of radar-controlled night-fighting tactics, but Kammhuber was most reluctant to consider their ideas. Maj Hans-Joachim Herrmann, a distinguished bomber pilot, proposed the re-introduction of

Below:
When *Jagdgeschwader 300* was formed in July 1943 as the first *Wilde Sau* unit, only sufficient single-engined fighters were available to equip its *I Gruppe*. II/JG 300 and III/JG 300 were forced to 'borrow' the dayfighters of III/JG 11 and II/JG 1. A Fw190A-3 of the latter unit is pictured.
Bundesarchiv 361/2193/32

Right:
Maj Heinz-Wolfgang Schnaufer (fourth from right) — pictured during an inspection by *Reichsmarschall* Hermann Göring — was the top-scoring nightfighter pilot with 121 victories to his credit. Bundesarchiv 659/6428/20

single-seat fighters into the night battle arena. He argued that these could be concentrated over the bombers' target, using searchlight illumination for target acquisition. Codenamed *Wilde Sau* (Wild Boar), this method was first tried on the night of 3 July during a raid on Cologne. Herrmann and nine other pilots claimed 12 enemy bombers destroyed, although their claims were disputed by the local flak commander. In theory, when the *Wilde Sau* fighters were operating, flak should have

been restricted to heights below 20,000ft, but on that occasion there had been a breakdown in communications. Clearly *Wilde Sau* tactics had little place in the orderly and scientific night defence system advocated by Kammhuber. Little more congenial to him were the ideas of Ob Viktor von Lossberg. Lossberg's tactics, which became known as *Zahme Sau* (Tame Boar) involved the use of radar-equipped nightfighters on freelance missions. They were to be directed into the bomber stream, where they could use their radars to find targets for themselves. Kammhuber was unconvinced that these methods would result in any worthwhile results, as he believed that without close ground control the fighters would be unable to locate the bombers. He was also concerned about the potential dangers of two uncontrolled fighter forces operating in the same airspace.

The resolution of this debate on tactics became a matter of extreme urgency in July 1943, when the RAF introduced 'Window' jamming during the Battle of Hamburg. 'Window' (a codename for metal foil strips) was an effective means of jamming both ground control and airborne radars and so at a stroke the defences of the Kammhuber Line were neutralised. The RAF despatched over 3,000 bomber sorties to Hamburg in the course of four raids and lost only 87 aircraft to the defences (an attrition rate of only 2.8%). Kammhuber had little option but to authorise the implementation of the *Wilde Sau* and *Zahme Sau* tactics. However, he saw this simply as a temporary measure to bridge the gap until jam-proof ground and airborne radars became available. He therefore ordered that the *Himmelbett* zones penetrated by the bomber

stream attempt to carry out interception by the traditional methods. They did in fact achieve some victories after July 1943, but these were usually against isolated stragglers from the bomber stream. The freelance night-fighting methods were much more successful and in August 1943 a record 250 victories were gained. Kammhuber's position was hopelessly undermined and in September he was replaced as commander of *Fliegerkorps XII* by Gen-Maj Josef 'Beppo' Schmid.

The clouds of 'Window' dropped by the RAF bombers did not prevent the German radars from following the course of the bomber stream (although it effectively prevented them from tracking individual aircraft). Therefore a running commentary could be broadcast by the controller, which would enable the *Zahme Sau* fighters to infiltrate the stream on its way to and from the target. The *Wilde Sau* fighters also used this method to concentrate over the target, but Herrmann wisely distrusted becoming reliant solely on these broadcasts and instiuted a separate system of visual signals to direct his single-engined fighters. The freelance fighter aircraft would initially assemble over visual and radio beacons, before they were directed on to the bombers. It was an extremely flexible system, as instead of being tied to rigid zones, fighters from every nightfighter base could be concentrated against the bombers. It seemed that in seeking to defeat the German nightfighters, the RAF had unwittingly forced them to adopt a far more efficient *modus operandi*. However, the freelance method of night-fighting had its weaknesses, which Bomber Command was not slow to exploit. As interception over the target was so important a feature of the new system, the RAF bombers shortened their time over the target to some 15-20min. And, since early identification of the target was also important for the direction of *Wilde Sau* fighters, the British sought to deny this information to the German controllers for as long as possible. This was achieved by hiding the bomber stream by radar jamming and by sending in 'spoof' raids, which sometimes completely fooled the enemy controllers. Finally, control at least of the *Zahme Sau* fighters depended on ground-to-air R/T communication and this could be jammed or 'spoofed' by German-speaking RAF controllers.

A notable example of the successful use of 'spoof' tactics by Bomber Command is offered by the raid on the Peenemünde research establishment on the night of 17/18 August 1943. A diversionary

raid on Berlin by Mosquito light bombers deceived the German controllers into identifying the German capital as the main forces' target. Consequently the nightfighters were slow to react to the real threat and only 44 RAF bombers were lost, as were 12 of the defending fighters. But had the Luftwaffe fighters been able to concentrate over the actual target, the RAF's losses on a clear, moonlit night would certainly have been considerable. The inexperienced Lt Dieter Musset of *II/NJG 1* was able to carry out attacks on six RAF bombers that night and at least four of them were destroyed by him. Taking off at 23.47hrs from St Trond, he was directed towards Berlin. However, noticing enemy activity to the north, he flew towards Peenemünde, where fires from the bombing were then blazing. The first of his targets was picked up on radar by his

Below:
This No 115 Squadron Lancaster II, based at East Wretham, had its rear turret shot away by a pair of Fw190s during a raid on Cologne, 28/29 June 1943. That night 25 bombers failed to return from a force of 608 despatched. IWM CE79

Above:
Messerschmitt Bf109G-6 of *I/JG 302* pictured during a detachment to Helsinki-Malmi airfield in Finland between 13/14 February and 1 May 1944. During this period the unit operated with the fighter control ship *Togo* which was based at Reval, Estonia. GQ, Finnish Army 146001

operator, Obgef Helmut Hafner, and Musset sent it down in flames with two bursts of fire. But so good was the visibility over the target that all the remaining contacts were picked up visually by the pilot. As Musset was able to pick out the bombers' exhausts from above, he could compensate for his Bf110's slow speed by attacking in a shallow dive from above. His sixth potential victim, an Avro Lancaster, fought back and its rear gunner succeeded in setting the Bf110's port engine alight. Musset tried to bring his fighter down, but was forced to give up the attempt and he and Hafner took to their parachutes.

The early successes of the *Wilde Sau* fighters led to a rapid build-up of the single-seat nightfighter units. The original *Wilde Sau Geschwader* (*Jagdgeschwader 300*) had formed at Bonn-Hangelar in July. But only *I/JG 300* had its own fighters, the *II* and *III Gruppen* being forced to borrow aircraft from dayfighter units. Inevitably this arrangement led to friction. Yet, once the *Wilde Sau* concept had been proved, not only were sufficient aircraft allocated to equip *JG 300* fully, but two new *Jagdgeschwader* (*JG 301* and *JG 302* were formed) in September 1943. By October, though, the RAF's countermeasures were beginning to bite. On 3/4 October, Bomber Command raided Kassel in force, but lost only 24 bombers to the defenders. A thoroughgoing reorganisation of the Reich's air defences seemed long overdue, more especially since the USAAF had now begun to penetrate

German airspace by day. *Fliegerkorps XII* was disbanded and in its place *Jadgkorps I* was created to control both day- and nightfighters. The only exception was made for Herrmann's *Wilde Sau* units, which as *Jagddivision 30* were subordinated to Luftwaffe Command Centre. Both day- and nightfighters became the responsibility of Adolf Galland, the *General der Jagdflieger*, Kammhuber then losing his position as General of Night Fighters which he had retained after his dismissal from command of *Fliegerkorps XII*.

The Luftwaffe's response to the RAF's introduction of 'spoof' tactics and its intensification of the radio countermeasures war was to improve the ground control system and to look for detection aids which were not liable to be jammed. The accuracy of raid plotting was improved and the ground observer network assumed a new importance pending the introduction of new 'jam-proof' radars. Even with their ground radars jammed, the Luftwaffe had received early warning of an impending raid from the monitoring of the RAF bombers' H2S radar test transmissions. The volume

of such testing would also give some indication of
the scale of the coming night's effort. The RAF
bombers' use of radar aids also gave the German
nightfighters the opportunity to home on to them
using passive (ie non-transmitting) homing devices.
The *Flensburg* equipment homed on to the British
Monica tail-warning radar, while *Naxos* detected
H2S emissions; the *Spanner* infra-red detection
system was also briefly reintroduced. The use of
such passive devices rendered the RAF Bomber
Support fighters' Serrate homing equipment ineffective. The best hope for an improvement in
airborne target detection, however, lay with the
Lichtenstein SN-2 radar, first test-flown in September 1943. By May 1944, 1,000 *SN-2* sets had been
delivered. Because this radar worked on a
frequency as yet unjammed by 'Window', its
introduction, together with the fitting of anti-
jamming devices to ground early warning and
fighter direction radars, enabled a return to
controlled night-fighting. However, valuable
lessons had been learnt from the experience of
freelance methods and the new tactics were far
more flexible than the rigid *Himmelbett* system,
finally abandoned in the autumn of 1943.

On 19/20 November 1943 Bomber Command
opened the Battle of Berlin, hoping to repeat the
success of the Hamburg raids against the German
capital. The winter weather created especially
serious problems for the single-engined fighters of
Herrmann's *Jagddivision 30* and many aircraft were

lost in crashes. Yet by the end of the year, there
were signs that the nightfighters were gaining the
advantage in the electronic battle of wits over
Germany. The RAF's deep penetration of enemy
air space worked to its disadvantage, giving the
Luftwaffe better opportunities to engage, and its
operational effectiveness was also hampered by
poor weather conditions. By the spring of 1944 the
Nachtjagdgruppen were clearly in the ascendant.
The new command and control system was, in the
words of a British assessment 'a formidable
defensive organisation with few weaknesses capable of exploitation'. The nightfighter force had
grown in strength by some 50% in the year
following the Hamburg battles, and during 1944
improved versions of the Ju88 finally superseded
the veteran Bf110, although the latter type
remained in service in substantial numbers right up
until the end of the war. Another notable
improvement was in aircraft armament, with the
widespread use of heavy calibre cannon and the
'*Schräge Musik*' (the German term for jazz)
installation of upward-angled cannon. The latter
device allowed the nightfighter to sit below a

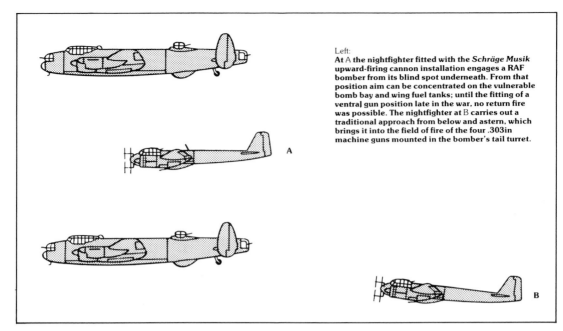

Left:
At A the nightfighter fitted with the *Schräge Musik* upward-firing cannon installation engages a RAF bomber from its blind spot underneath. From that position aim can be concentrated on the vulnerable bomb bay and wing fuel tanks; until the fitting of a ventral gun position late in the war, no return fire was possible. The nightfighter at B carries out a traditional approach from below and astern, which brings it into the field of fire of the four .303in machine guns mounted in the bomber's tail turret.

Bomber Attack Tactics — 1944

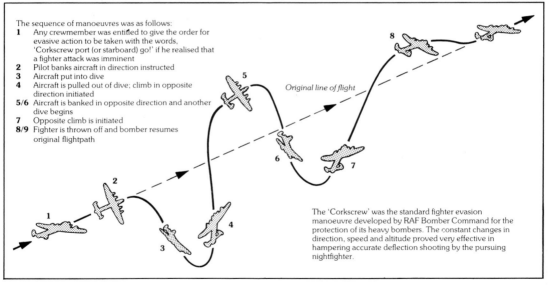

The sequence of manoeuvres was as follows:
1 Any crewmember was entitled to give the order for evasive action to be taken with the words, 'Corkscrew port (or starboard) go!' if he realised that a fighter attack was imminent
2 Pilot banks aircraft in direction instructed
3 Aircraft put into dive
4 Aircraft is pulled out of dive; climb in opposite direction initiated
5/6 Aircraft is banked in opposite direction and another dive begins
7 Opposite climb is initiated
8/9 Fighter is thrown off and bomber resumes original flightpath

Original line of flight

The 'Corkscrew' was the standard fighter evasion manoeuvre developed by RAF Bomber Command for the protection of its heavy bombers. The constant changes in direction, speed and altitude proved very effective in hampering accurate deflection shooting by the pursuing nightfighter.

The 'Corkscrew' Evasion Manoeuvre

bomber, in its blind spot, and pump shells into the vulnerable wing fuel tanks or bomb bay.

The German nightfighting successes were reflected in a rising toll of RAF bomber casualties, which culminated in two especially disastrous raids. On 24/25 March 1944, 72 out of a total of 810 bombers raiding Berlin failed to return and, on 30/31 March, 95 bombers out of a force of 795 despatched to Nuremberg were reported missing. The latter losses, Bomber Command's worst of the war, represented an attrition rate of over 11.9%. A number of special conditions led to these exceptionally heavy losses: visibility was especially good that night, the German controllers were not taken in

Luftwaffe Nightfighter Force March 1944

Unit	Base	Aircraft
1. Jagddivision	Döberitz	
I /NJG 5	Stendal	Bf110
II /NJG 5	Parchim	Bf110
III /NJG 5	Brandis	Bf110
IV/NJG 5	Erfurt	Bf110
I /JG 300	Jüterborg	Bf109
II /JG 300	Ludwiglust	Bf109
III /JG 300	Brandis	Bf109
IV /JG 300	Erfurt	Bf109
Nachtjagdgruppe 10	Werneuchen	Various
	Bonn-Hangelar	
2. Jagddivision	Stade	
I /NJG 3	Vechta	Bf110
II /NJG 3	Vechta	Ju88
III /NJG 3	Stade	Bf110
IV /NJG 3	Westerland	Ju88, Bf110
III /JG 301	Oldenburg	Bf109, Fw190
3. Jagddivision	Deelen	
I /NJG 1	Venlo	Bf110, He219
IV/NJG 1	St Trond	Bf110
I /NJG 2	Bad Langensalza	Ju88
II /NJG 2	Quackenbrück	Ju88
III /NJG 2	Langendiebach	Ju88
	Twente	
III /NJG 4	Mainz-Finthen	Bf110
I /JG 300	Bonn-Hangelar	Bf109
II /JG 300	Rheine	Fw190
III /JG 300	Wiesbaden	Bf109
4. Jagddivision	Chantilly	
II /NJG 1	St Dizier	Bf110
III /NJG 1	Laon-Athies	Bf110
I /NJG 4	Florennes	Bf109
II /NJG 4	Coulommiers	Bf109
7. Jagddivision	Schleissheim	
I /NJG 6	Mainz-Finthen	Bf110
II /NJG 6	Stuttgart-Echterdingen	Bf110
I /JG 301	Neuburg	Bf109

by diversionary 'spoof' raids, and the well tried tactics of evasive routeing for the main bomber force were for some inexplicable reason ignored by the RAF. Nonetheless, it was a tremendous victory for the renascent *Nachtjagdgruppen*. As one German pilot reported 'normally our biggest problem was to find the bomber stream, but on this night we had no trouble'. Oblt Martin Becker of

Below:
A captured He219A-7 on display at RAE Farnborough in the autumn of 1945. This aircraft was evaluated by the Central Fighter Establishment at Tangmere, which had by that time absorbed the Fighter Interception Unit (FIU) as part of its Nightfighter Development Wing. IWM MH4881

Above:
On 9 April 1945 *I/NJG 1* had 22 Heinkel He219s on strength, but most were grounded due to shortage of fuel. The *1. Staffel* aircraft illustrated was deliberately wrecked before its airfield was overrun by American troops. IWM MH13495

I/NJG 6, flying a Bf110, was especially successful, gaining seven confirmed victories during the course of two sorties that night.

Bomber Command largely abandoned deep-penetration raids in April, confirming its main effort to comparatively short-penetration targets outlined by the 'Transportation Plan' in support of the forthcoming Normandy invasion. However, pressure on the German defences was maintained through harassing raids on Berlin by Mosquitos of

single-engined fighters of *JG 300*, *JG 301* and *JG 302* were drawn into the daylight battles over the Reich against the USAAF's heavy bombers.

An event of some significance occurred on the night of 15/16 June, when Helmut Lent, Kommodore of *NJG 3* shot down three Lancasters to bring his total of night victories up to 100. He was the first pilot to do so and only Schnaufer exceeded his record. One of the pioneer night-fighting pilots with *II/NJG 1*, Lent was killed in a flying accident early in October 1944. By mid-1944 the *Nachtjagdgruppen* had become indisputably the most effective arm of the Luftwaffe, but from then onwards its decline was rapid. Many of the causes for this were beyond its control. Like the rest of the Luftwaffe, it was hampered by acute fuel shortages which not only curtailed operations but also affected the supply of trained replacement crews. The Allied armies' advance in the West denied the nightfighters their essential early-warning facility and also restricted their room for manoeuvre. By pure mischance, the RAF was enabled to introduce effective jamming of the *SN-2* radar, when a Ju88G fitted with this equipment landed in error at Woodbridge in Suffolk on 13 July. As the Luftwaffe had short-sightedly neglected the further development of new radars — and especially those operating on centimetric wavelengths — the jamming of *SN-2* was a very

the Light Night Striking Force. The Mosquito proved to be a particularly elusive target: even the new He219 nightfighter lacked the performance to catch it and the Focke-Wulf Ta154 — envisaged as a 'Mosquito hunter' — never got into service. Single-engined nightfighters were also pressed into service as Mosquito hunters, at a time when their effectiveness by night was generally waning. One of the most successful pilots in this role was Oblt Kurt Welter of *JG 300*, who later led the Luftwaffe's first jet nightfighter unit. His ultimate total of 61 victories included no fewer than 35 Mosquitos. Increasingly though, from the spring of 1944 onwards the

Below:
The secrets of *Lichtenstein SN-2* (and of the *Flensburg* and *Naxos* passive homing systems) were compromised when this Ju88G of *III/NJG 2* landed in error at Woodbridge in Suffolk on 13 July 1944. IWM HU2735

serious blow. Moreover, both the *Naxos* and *Flensburg* systems had been compromised by the Ju88G's capture and thereafter Bomber Command aircraft were sparing in their use of H2S and Monica. A return to infra-red detection with the *Kiel* device proved ultimately unprofitable and so the initiative in the radio countermeasures contest passed back to the RAF. However, one noteworthy technical development was the Luftwaffe's intro-

From mid-1944 onwards the Junkers Ju88G began to replace the Bf110 as the Luftwaffe's principal nightfighter type. It not only offered a considerable increase in performance, but also carried a more comprehensive range of electronic equipment.
IWM HU 2736

duction of an interference-free ground-to-air data transmission system.

Germany's failure to produce specialised night-fighter aircraft in adequate numbers also contributed to the ultimate defeat of the *Nachtjagdgruppen*. For, apart from relatively limited numbers of the He219s, the nightfighter units ended the war

This partially-dismantled Ju88G of *II/NJG 4* was captured at Wunstorf, near Hanover, in April 1945.
IWM BU3261

flying later developments of the Bf110 and Ju88 with which they had first been equipped in 1940. Nightfighter versions of the Ju388 and Do335 aircraft did not proceed beyond the experimental stage. Jet nightfighters based on the Arado Ar234 and Me262 were proposed, but only an improvised version of the latter saw even limited service. Sufficient two-seat Me262B trainers to equip a single *Staffel* were modified by the fitting of *FuG 218 Neptun* radar and they began operating in defence of Berlin in February 1945. At least eight Mosquitos were accounted for by this unit (*10/NJG11*) and three of these fell to the *Staffelkapitän*, Oblt Welter.

By the end of 1944 the *Nachtjagdgruppen* were overwhelmed by tactical problems. RAF Bomber Command's successful use of radio-countermeasures and 'spoof' tactics made interception very difficult. Moreover, RAF Intruder and Bomber Support operations were becoming increasingly effective. The use of Perfectos forced the Germans to switch off their IFF sets, thus making the exercise of effective ground control even more difficult. Under these conditions, the German nightfighters' preferred tactics were to infiltrate the bomber stream, where electronic interference would be limited and the dangers from RAF nightfighters much reduced. The problem — which was never satisfactorily resolved — was how to direct them there. In December 1944 the *Nachtjagdgruppen*, with a strength of nearly 1,000 operational aircraft, claimed only 66 victories, while during the same period they lost 114 of their own aircraft. Little impression could be made even against deep penetrations. On 13/14 February over 800 bombers carried out a devastatingly effective attack on Dresden and this was virtually unopposed. Indeed, in the course of 36 major operations by Bomber Command in January-March 1945, involving the despatch of 15,588 sorties, only 240 bombers were lost. Although isolated groups of nightfighter pilots fought bravely on to the end, the greater number of German nightfighters sat immobile on their airfields during the closing weeks of the war in Europe.

5 Baedeker Raids and the Baby Blitz

During the second half of 1941 bomber attacks against the UK continued at a low level of activity; the greater part of the Luftwaffe's bomber strength was committed to the campaign against the Soviet Union. The units of *Luftflotte 3* which remained in the West were mainly concerned with attacks on coastal ports and shipping and minelaying. Some raids were made on British cities at this time though. In July and August 1941, Birmingham and London were attacked and, in October, Manchester was raided, but on no occasion were more than 100 aircraft involved. This lull in the German bombing campaign could not be allowed to affect the rapid build-up of the RAF's night air defences, however. For it was far from clear that the Soviet Union would be able to withstand the German onslaught and, if the war against Russia had been the brief one envisaged by Hitler, large bomber forces would then have been released, enabling the resumption of the night Blitz on Britain.

Minelaying aircraft proved to be especially difficult targets to deal with, because of the AI Mk IV radar's poor performance at low level. The set's maximum range was governed by the altitude at which the nightfighter was flying, since returns of the radar pulses from the ground beneath the aircraft increasingly blotted out the radar picture at lower heights. When nightfighter and target were flying at about 15,000ft, the AI Mk IV's maximum

range was some 3-4 miles. But, with interceptor and target flying at 3,000ft, the maximum range had closed to only ½ mile and any bomber flying at a lower level was for all practical purposes immune from interception by AI Mk IV. Standard operational procedure was for the nightfighter to approach its target at a slightly lower level, so that it could more easily be picked out against the night sky when the fighter had got to within visual range. (The theoretical minimum range of 800ft for AI Mk IV, proved to be about 1,000ft to 1,200ft in practice.) Therefore, very precise ground control was needed if a nightfighter was to be directed into contact with a low-flying target. And, if the nightfighter pilot miscalculated his turn on to the enemy bomber's course, or if the quarry began evasive manoeuvring, contact would soon be lost as the target passed beyond AI range.

It was found that the best method of intercepting a low-flying enemy aircraft was for the nightfighter to approach from above rather than below. Flt Lt J. R. D. Braham of No 29 Squadron, flying with his

Below:
The Beaufighter VIf which entered service early in 1942 was fitted with more powerful Hercules VI or XVI radial engines, and offered an appreciable improvement in performance over the earlier Beaufighter nightfighter marks. IWM CH15213

usual radar operator (RO), Sgt W. J. Gregory, had a successful combat using this method in October 1941. His Beaufighter was scrambled from West Malling and vectored on to an enemy aircraft approaching the Thames Estuary at low level. Braham climbed up to 8,000ft and was advised that his target was 4,000ft below. The Beaufighter was directed into position astern of the enemy aircraft, before Braham began to lose height. He did this in gradual increments, at the same time closing the range. At a range of 1½ miles Gregory picked up an AI contact, well below and to port; following his instructions, Braham continued to let down, 500ft at a time, and turned-in dead astern of the contact. At 4,500ft altitude he picked out the enemy bomber about 500ft below him, skimming above a cloud layer. Range had by then closed to 1,200ft — virtually the AI Mk IV's minimum. Identifying the target as a Do217, Braham fired a 2-3sec burst into it with cannon and machine guns and saw the enemy dive through the clouds. Shortly afterwards he saw an explosion on the surface of the sea. A combination of good tactics and very skilful flying could produce results against low-flying raiders. But clearly they were not full substitutes for more effective radar equipment, especially since the

Principal RAF Fighter Command Nightfighter Airfields — 1942-45

Above:
No 307 (Polish) Squadron began to convert from the Defiant to the Beaufighter IIf in August 1941 and was operational on the new aircraft by October. The squadron was based at Exeter from April 1941 until April 1943. Polish Institute and Sikorski Museum

Luftwaffe was, by late 1941, fully aware of the protection it gained by operating at low level.

Re-equipment of the nightfighter force continued apace during the latter part of 1941. By the end of the year 12 squadrons were equipped with the Beaufighter for service in the UK and a further Beaufighter squadron (No 89 Squadron) had been despatched to Egypt. Moreover, the early Beaufighter I and II, powered respectively by 1,500hp Hercules XI and 1,280hp Merlin XX powerplants, were being replaced by the more powerful Beaufighter VI fitted with 1,670hp Hercules V1 engines. Seven nightfighter squadrons flew the unsatisfactory Defiant at the end of 1941, for want of more suitable equipment. An attempt had been made to improve the aircraft's night-fighting capabilities by installing an AI radar, but, since the controls of the AI Mk IV could not be fitted in the Defiant's turret because of lack of space, the pilot-operated AI Mk VI developed for single-seat fighters was instead installed. Two squadrons flew AI Mk VI Defiants (Nos 96 and 264), but they were not a success and in any case the Defiant lacked adequate performance for the night-fighting role. By mid-1942 the Defiant had been retired from frontline service. Five squadrons converted to the Beaufighter (a sixth new Beaufighter unit, No 488 Squadron RNZAF reformed with the type in June 1942), while the other two Defiant squadrons received Mosquitos.

The Mosquito II, which entered service in January 1942, offered a tremendous improvement in performance over the Beaufighter. Its maximum speed of 370mph at 14,000ft was nearly 40mph higher than that of the Beaufighter VI, while its service ceiling of 34,500ft bettered the latter aircraft's 26,500ft ceiling by a considerable margin.

It was moreover less tricky to fly and more manoeuvrable than the Beaufighter, although the latter's initial rate-of-climb was much better. Armed with four 20mm cannon and four .303in machine guns, the Mosquito II carried either AI Mk IV or AI Mk V radar. The latter was essentially similar to AI Mk IV, but had an additional indicator mounted at the pilot's position. No 157 Squadron, formed at Debden on 13 December 1941, was the first unit to receive the new nightfighter, becoming operational in April 1942. By June the two former Defiant units, Nos 151 and 264 Squadrons, were also operational on Mosquitos. At the end of 1941, No 85 Squadron was alone in operating AI Mk IV-equipped Douglas Havocs in the defensive nightfighter role. However, 10 flights (later to be expanded to full squadron strength) operated the unsuccessful 'Turbinlite' Havocs. No 85 Squadron's aircraft, which carried a nose-mounted armament of eight .303in machine guns, were somewhat more successful than the Turbinlites. Between April 1941 and September 1942 Havoc crews claimed 12 enemy aircraft destroyed, plus two shared victories, eight probables and 16 enemy aircraft damaged. Nevertheless, the Havoc's performance was really inadequate for the role and in August 1942 No 85 Squadron began re-equipping with Mosquitos.

Further progress in the development of AI radar was being made during the early months of 1942, leading to the introduction of the AI Mk VII and AI

Mk VIII 'centrimetric' radars. They operated in the 10cm waveband, rather than AI Mk IV's 1½m waveband, hence the term 'centrimetric'. The shorter operating waveband allowed the use of much smaller transmitting and receiving aerials than those needed for AI Mk IV. Indeed, by the use of electronic switching, the same aerial was in fact used for both transmitting and receiving. This much more compact arrangement permitted a reflector dish to be fitted behind the aerial, which focused the signals into a relatively narrow 12° beam. An appreciable increase in maximum acquisition range was thereby obtained. That for the AI Mk VII, the initial version of the centrimetric radar which only

went into limited production, was 6 miles and the AI Mk VIII's went up to 8 miles. Furthermore, the AI Mk IV's problems with 'clutter' from ground returns at low level was very much reduced, because apart from some 'spillage' no signals were transmitted downwards. The narrower beam also improved the accuracy of target tracking. However, had it been fixed to point straight ahead from the aircraft's centreline, its coverage would have been much too narrow for practical target acquisition. Accordingly, the coverage was increased by oscillating and revolving the reflector dish so that the beam scanned a cone 30° in elevation and azimuth from the centreline. The new radar was obviously the

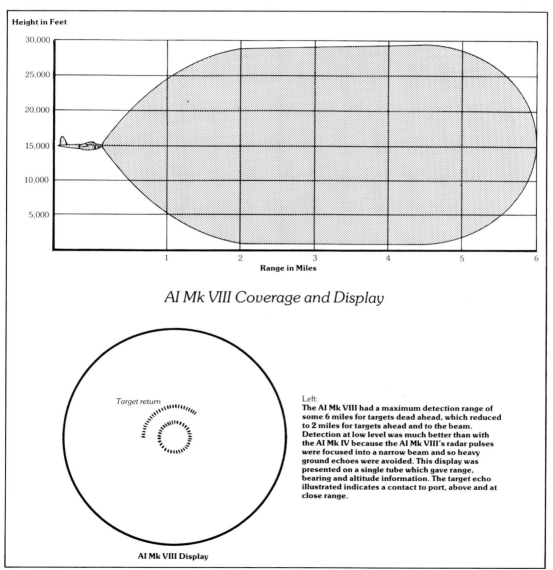

AI Mk VIII Coverage and Display

AI Mk VIII Display

Left:
The AI Mk VIII had a maximum detection range of some 6 miles for targets dead ahead, which reduced to 2 miles for targets ahead and to the beam. Detection at low level was much better than with the AI Mk IV because the AI Mk VIII's radar pulses were focused into a narrow beam and so heavy ground echoes were avoided. This display was presented on a single tube which gave range, bearing and altitude information. The target echo illustrated indicates a contact to port, above and at close range.

Left:
With the fitting of AI Mk VII and VIII centimetric radar to the Beaufighter the nightfighters' ability to detect low-flying targets was greatly improved. The first service trials with the new equipment were carried out early in 1942 and here involve Beaufighter I X7624. BAe

answer to the problems of intercepting low level radars. The first success was gained on 5 April 1942 by a Beaufighter of the FIU. But it was June before centimetric radar began to reach the squadrons and by that time the Luftwaffe's *'Baedeker'* raids were well under way.

The limited capacity of the GCI stations was another problem which needed attention. As each could only direct one nightfighter at a time, only three or four interceptions an hour were possible at best. Measures were put in hand to increase the number of control positions at each station. Instead of just one controller dealing with one nightfighter, it was intended to have two controllers each carrying out two interceptions at the same time. A third controller would be available to off-load the work of identifying and allocating targets, liaison with sector control and general management of the GCI station. In the meantime, nightfighters not under GCI control could carry out freelance patrols in co-operation with searchlights — a procedure which had been considerably refined since first tried out during the Blitz. Sufficient searchlights were

Below:
Beaufighter VIf V8565 of the FIU is seen fitted with AI Mk VIII radar. The FIU gained the first operational success with centimetric AI on 5 April 1942, when a low-flying Do217 was brought down. IWM CH16668

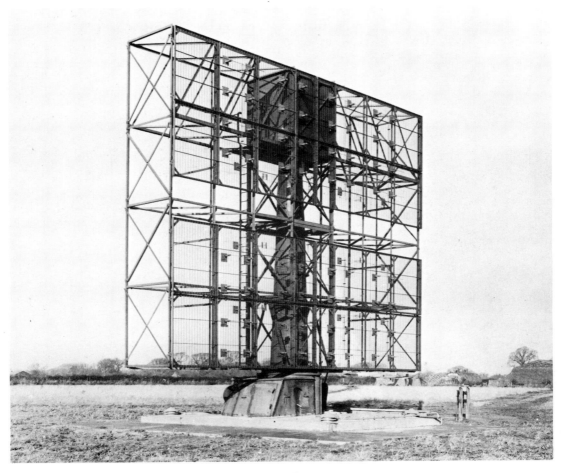

available by the beginning of 1942 to create a series of illuminated 'Fighter Boxes' covering most of southern England and the Midlands. The comparatively low-powered 90cm lights were positioned in an Indicator Zone and were responsible for pointing towards, but not necessarily actually illuminating, a target. Behind these the newer 150cm lights were grouped in a 'Killer Zone' and sufficiently closely spaced to provide continuous illumination of the enemy aircraft. Many of the searchlights were by that time radar-directed. Thus a patrolling night-fighter received a good indication of the position of a raider and, once it had been picked up on AI, the searchlights could be instructed to switch off.

In the first three months of 1942 the Luftwaffe confined its night raiding to small-scale efforts against coastal targets. Then Hitler, stung by an especially damaging attack by RAF Bomber Command on Lübeck, ordered that raids on Britain be intensified and that 'besides raids on ports and industry, terror attacks of a retaliatory nature are to be carried out against towns other than London'.

Above:
The GCI radar station at Orby in Lincolnshire. In the foreground is the rotating radar aerial, with the camouflaged operations building behind it. This Type VII set could detect targets flying at 5,000ft at 20 miles range, while high-flying aircraft were detectable at 90 miles. IWM

The 'Baedeker' raids — so-called by both sides because their targets were often small towns of cultural and historical importance listed in the prewar Baedeker Guides — began on 23/24 April. Exeter was the objective for that night, but poor visibility hampered the bombing which was widely scattered. The following night Exeter was again the target for an attack delivered in two waves, with about 25 bombers in each. Over 100 defensive sorties were flown, but the RAF nightfighters only shot down three enemy bombers. As many of the targets in this offensive were of minor military importance, they were unprotected by balloon barrages, enabling attacks to be made from low

Top:
In the course of a *'Baedeker'* raid or- Exeter on the night of 3/4 May 1942, No 307 Squadron's Beaufighters claimed four enemy aircraft destroyed. One crew — Sgt Illaszewicz and Plt Off Lissowski — accounted for two German bombers that night.
Polish Institute and Sikorski Museum

Above:
Three of the RAF's most successful nightfighter pilots served together on No 85 Squadron at Hunsdon in 1943. Sqn Ldr Peter Green (left) was O/C 'A' Flight, Wg Cdr John Cunningham (centre) commanded the squadron, and Sqn Ldr Edward Crew was O/C 'B' Flight. IWM CH9534

level. During the particularly destructive raids on Bath, which were carried out on 25/26 April and 26/27 April, bombers were reported to have come down as low as 600ft. The nightfighters, still equipped with AI Mk IV, found it extremely difficult to locate the low-flying raiders. Moreover, the defenders' problems were compounded by the concentrated nature of the attacks, generally lasting about half an hour, since the capacity of the GCI stations was still so limited. On the night of 28/29 April the Turbinlite Havoc went into action for the first time during a raid on York. An illuminating aircraft from No 1459 Flight, operating with a Hurricane of No 253 Squadron, contacted an enemy aircraft and held it briefly in its searchlight beam. However, before the Hurricane could set up its attack, the German took evasive action and made good his escape. Two nights later a Turbinlite Havoc and a Hurricane from the same two units contacted a He111 and the fighter pilot was able to pick out the enemy aircraft without the need for searchlight illumination. His attack brought the enemy bomber down into the sea off Flamborough Head — it was, though, an uncharacteristic success. In September 1942 the Turbinlite flights were each combined with a Hurricane flight to form Nos 530 to 539 Squadrons, rather than as hitherto operating with a fighter squadron. But the Turbinlite concept had been shown by experience to be unworkable and these units were disbanded in January 1943.

In the meantime even the well conceived radar-controlled night-fighting tactics were scarcely working against the 'Baedeker' raids. On the night of 3/4 May the Luftwaffe returned to Exeter to carry out a very damaging raid. No 307 (Polish) Squadron, based at Exeter airfield, were equipped with Beaufighter Mk IIs fitted with AI Mk IV. In view of the limitations of this equipment in detecting low-flying bombers, the Polish crews did well to claim four enemy aircraft destroyed. On 8/9 May, Norwich was the target, but unusually the Luftwaffe chose a moonless night for the raid and the bombing went badly astray. No 85 Squadron, operating from Hunsdon, gained seven radar contacts that night, but such was the poor performance of their Havocs that none could be converted into enemy aircraft destroyed. Sqn Ldr Maude was patrolling at 10,000ft, when his RO, Flt Sgt Cairns, obtained a contact at 00.15hrs. The enemy aircraft was flying at a higher altitude and flying a weaving course as an evasive tactic. The Havoc, flying at 270mph, was unable to close the range beyond 4,000ft and eventually the contact was lost. An hour later this crew obained a chance contact 40 miles off Orfordness. However, the enemy aircraft was approaching head-on and, as Maude turned in behind it, radar contact was lost. The experience of Flt Lt Howitt and his RO, Flg Off McInnes, was even more frustrating: patrolling at 11,000ft, they obtained five contacts, all of which were below. On the first two occasions contact was lost as the enemy aircraft drew away. Then three targets were picked up, but the one selected for pursuit showed the IFF response of a friendly aircraft.

Fighter Command's newer aircraft were beginning to achieve a better success rate, though. On the night of 24/25 June, Birmingham was the Luftwaffe's target, although the attack went so badly astray that not a single bomb hit the city. No 151 Squadron's Mosquitos, based at Wittering, were sent up against the raiders. The CO, Wg Cdr I. S. Smith DFC, contacted a He111 flying at 8,000ft and closed in to attack; just as he was about to open fire, his Mosquito was spotted and the

Below:
In November 1942 the Beaufighter VIfs of No 600 Squadron were despatched overseas to North Africa in support of the 'Torch' landings. The unit remained in the Mediterranean theatre until the end of the war. IWM CH17800

enemy bomber dived away. Nevertheless, Smith was able to get in two bursts before the Heinkel disappeared into cloud; it was assessed as probably destroyed. Ten minutes after this combat, at 23.40hrs, the same Mosquito was directed on to a Do217. Smith closed in to 100yd unseen and then fired a very short burst of cannon fire — the German bomber dived down into the sea. This was the first confirmed victory credited to a Mosquito. A second confirmed success followed within minutes, when Smith contacted another Do217: his opening burst set it alight and, evading the bomber's return fire, Smith fired a further burst to deliver the *coup de grâce*. On the same night a second Mosquito from No 151 Squadron made two contacts, but was unable to claim any damage to the two German bombers.

By midsummer the steady, if unspectacular, successes of the British night defences had begun to take their effect on the already small Luftwaffe bomber force in the West. The rate of losses was by then much greater than the flow of replacement bomber crews from the training organisation could hope to replace. Late in July the bombers raided Birmingham on three nights and on 31 July/1 August attacked Hull, losing 27 bombers in the process. Thereafter, the night attacks were mounted on a much smaller scale. During August and September the targets were Norwich (attacked twice), Swansea, Colchester (attacked twice), Ipswich, Portsmouth, Sunderland and King's Lynn; but on no occasion did the bombing force exceed 20 aircraft. The last raid of the 'Baedeker' series came on 31 October/1 November, when Canterbury was the target. The attack, following up a daylight raid by fighter-bombers, was flown in two waves with a 4hr separation between the two which

allowed the crews to fly double sorties. The bombing was not well concentrated and seven of the raiders failed to return. No 29 Squadron's Beaufighters, flying from West Malling, were particularly successful: one crew, Flg Off G. Pepper and his RO, Plt Off J. H. Toone (inevitably nicknamed 'Salt'), shot down three bombers during two sorties that night and a fourth enemy aircraft fell to the highly-skilled team of Braham and Gregory.

The 'Baedeker' raids had certainly highlighted the problems of low-altitude interception, which the nightfighters by themselves were unable to solve until equipped with the new 'centimetric' radar. However, low altitude bombing had only been possible because the selected targets lacked balloon barrage and AA artillery defences. Once these had been deployed, the Luftwaffe's bombers were forced up to bombing altitudes where the nightfighters were better able to deal with them. The final blow to the 'Baedeker' offensive came in November with the Allied 'Torch' landings in North Africa, which caused the German High Command to redeploy its bomber forces to take account of the new threat.

By mid-1943 six Beaufighter squadrons had converted to the Mosquito (Nos 25, 29, 410, 256 and 307) and a further two Mosquito Intruder units were available to reinforce the night defences in an emergency. Eight squadrons continued to fly the Beaufighters, all having by then converted to the

Mk VI fitted with AI Mk VIII centimetric radar. Another four Beaufighter nightfighter squadrons had been despatched to North Africa from the UK. The first Mosquitos to carry AI Mk VIII radar reached No 85 Squadron during the spring of 1943; a 'thimble' radome installation was fitted in the aircraft's nose, this necessitating the deletion of the four .303in machine guns. Some concern had been voiced about this reduction in armament, but No 85 Squadron's CO, Wg Cdr John Cunningham, enthusiastically reported that the new radar more than compensated for the loss of the machine guns. Mosquito IIs fitted with AI Mk VIII were designated NF XIIs, while a similar installation in FB VIs (which had provision for underwing droptanks) became NF XIIIs. The widespread use of centimetric radar led to a modification of interception techniques — instead of the controller directing the nightfighter into a position astern of the target, as was necessary with AI Mk IV and Mk V-equipped aircraft, he would direct the fighter into contact as soon as possible. He then left the AI operator (by this time usually known as the navigator, rather than the RO) to direct the turn on to the target's course. Thus by handing over responsibility for the interception at an earlier stage, GCI controllers were able to increase the number of nightfighters they could handle. Another advantage of the new technique was discovered when the Luftwaffe began using fast fighter-bomber aircraft at night. For if the night-fighter had little or no speed advantage over its opponent, it could be directed into a head-on interception. Then providing the navigator judged his turn on to the target's tail well, a long and possibly fruitless stern chase would be avoided.

The Luftwaffe's bomber forces in the West had recovered sufficient strength by mid-January 1943 to carry out the largest raid on London since the end of the night Blitz. On 17/18 January a two-wave attack, amounting to 118 sorties, dropped about 115 tons of bombs aimed at the East End docks. Many bombs fell short of the target area and six bombers failed to return. The lion's share of the defensive action again went to No 29 Squadron's Beaufighters and the squadron flew 27 sorties that night. Flt Sgt Wood had an inconclusive encounter with a Ju88, but Flg Off A. Musgrove and Sgt J. Petrie were more fortunate, seeing the Ju88 that they attacked going down in flames. Wg Cdr C. M. Wight-Boycott, then nearing the end of his tour in command of the squadron, flew twice that night and gained victories on both sorties. He and his navigator, Flg Off E. A. Sanders, were already airborne on a training exercise when they were directed into an interception of a Do217. Wight-Boycott sent the German bomber diving into the sea off Folkestone and briefly engaged a second, before returning to West Malling to refuel. In the

RAF Fighter Command Nightfighter Squadrons June 1943		
Squadron	Aircraft	Base
No 25 Squadron	Mosquito NF II	Church Fenton
No 29 Squadron	Beaufighter VIf	Bradwell Bay
No 68 Squadron	Beaufighter VIf	Coltishall
No 85 Squadron	Mosquito NF XII	West Malling
No 96 Squadron	Beaufighter VIf	Honiley
No 125 Squadron	Beaufighter VIf	Exeter
No 141 Squadron	Beaufighter VIf	Wittering
No 151 Squadron	Mosquito NF II	Colerne
No 157 Squadron	Mosquito NF II	Hunsdon
No 256 Squadron	Mosquito NF XII	Ford
No 264 Squadron	Mosquito NF II	Predannack
No 307 Squadron	Mosquito NF II	Fairwood Common
No 406 Squadron	Beaufighter VIf	Valley
No 409 Squadron	Beaufighter VIf	Acklington
No 410 Squadron	Mosquito NF II	Coleby Grange
No 418 Squadron	Boston III	Ford
No 456 Squadron	Mosquito NF II	Middle Wallop
No 488 Squadron	Beaufighter VIf	Ayr
No 604 Squadron	Beaufighter VIf	Scorton
No 605 Squadron	Mosquito NF II	Castle Camps
FIU	Mosquito and Beaufighter	Ford

course of his second sortie, Wight-Boycott engaged another three German bombers and claimed all of them as destroyed. For this feat, he was awarded the DSO.

A second large-scale attack was mounted against London on 3/4 March. A total of 117 bomber sorties were flown for the loss of six raiders, but few of the bombs found their target. The shortcomings thus revealed led to the appointment of Ob Dietrich Peltz as *Angriffsführer England* with special responsibilities for prosecuting the air war against Britain. His command included 135 bombers, as well as reconnaissance and fighter-bomber aircraft. Yet, although this appointment clearly presaged an intensification of night-bombing raids, sortie rates remained at a low level for the remainder of the year. However, new nightbomber aircraft appeared during this period, which were to present the defences with some problems. In August and September 1942 Ju86R high-altitude bombers had carried out daylight bombing raids from above 40,000ft. In anticipation of having to deal with this threat by night, a special variant of the Mosquito was produced; designated the Mosquito NF XV, it incorporated a pressure cabin for the crew and was fitted with AI Mk VIII. Armament comprised four .303in machine guns in a belly pack. The five aircraft produced were issued to No 85 Squadron at Hunsdon, forming 'C' Flight. From March 1943

they began practice interceptions, on one flight attaining a record altitude of 44,600ft. But since high altitude night attacks by Ju86s never in fact materialised, the Mosquito XVs were withdrawn from frontline service in August.

In mid-April 1943, Focke-Wulf Fw190 fighter-bombers of *Schnellkampfgeschwader 10* — which had been raiding British targets in daylight tip-and-run raids — began to operate at night. These extremely fast and manoeuvrable aircraft were believed to be virtually immune from interception by any RAF nightfighter then in service. But, conversely, the Luftwaffe fighter-bomber pilots found night operations very tricky. On *SKG 10's* first night raid on 16/17 April, 30 sorties were despatched against London, but such were the difficulties of navigation for the fighter-bombers that only two bombs landed on this massive target. And to compound this failure, six of the raiders failed to return. Three of them landed at West Malling, believing themselves in France, and a fourth

Above:
Mosquito NF XVII DZ659:H was the first to be fitted with the American SCR-720 centimetric radar, which was designated AI Mk X by the RAF. It is pictured in the markings of the FIU at Wittering, where the Unit moved in April 1944. IWM MH61152

crashed in attempting to get down on the same airfield. Despite these misadventures, *SKG 10* persevered with its night raiding. No 85 Squadron's Mosquito NF XIIs were re-deployed to West Malling in order to counter this threat and on the night of 16/17 May they convincingly exploded the myth of the Fw190's invulnerability by claiming four of them as destroyed. Sqn Ldr W. P. Green, Commander of 'A' Flight, was the first pilot to score, but Flg Off B. J. Thwaites not only gained a confirmed victory over a Fw190 later that night, but also claimed a second as probably destroyed. In fact, when loaded with two 66gal droptanks and a 550lb or 1,100lb bomb, the Fw190 lost its performance edge over the Mosquito.

A more formidable antagonist in many ways was the twin-engined Me410 *Schnellbomber* (fast bomber) which began operating against Britain in June. No 85 Squadron — which, having replaced No 29 Squadron at West Malling, was now itself getting a disproportionate share of action — scored the first victory against this type on 13/14 July. However, a much tougher combat with a Me410 was fought by Sqn Ldr W. H. Maguire on the night of 7/8 October 1943. Patrolling at 25,000ft, he was directed on to a contact flying at 9,000ft. As the Me410 was burning its navigation lights, Maguire soon gained visual contact as he rapidly lost height to engage. He was warned by control that a second enemy aircraft was flying a mile astern of his contact. When the Mosquito got 2,000ft behind the Me410, it began violent evasive action, attempting to get on to the RAF fighter's tail. However, the

Operation 'Steinbock' — January to May 1944					
Month	Sorties	Bomb Tonnage	Targets	German Losses	Attrition Rate (%)
January	732	426	London	57	7.88
February	1,386	1,082	London	72	5.2
March	909	755	London Hull Bristol	75	8.3
April	862	351	London Hull Bristol Portsmouth Plymouth	75	8.7
May	380	198	Bristol Portsmouth Weymouth Falmouth	approx 50	10

Mosquito eventually got the better of this turning fight and Maguire was able to fire two bursts of cannon fire into his opponent. The Me410 then turned and dived away, pursued by Maguire; he had the chance of firing just one more burst before the enemy aircraft dived into cloud. He saw nothing more of it, but another Mosquito crew reported flaming wreckage falling into the sea at the position of this last contact, south of Hastings. On the following night No 85 Squadron brought down the first Ju188 to fall to the British defences, this improved version of the Ju88 having only recently become operational with the Luftwaffe.

After Bomber Command instituted 'Window' jamming during the Battle of Hamburg in July, Fighter Command anticipated that the Luftwaffe bombers would introduce this countermeasure. Trials had shown that AI Mk VIII was especially vulnerable to 'Window' jamming. However, the American SCR720 radar, made available to Britain under Lease-Lend, was more jam-resistant. Designated AI Mk X, it was fitted to Mosquito NF II airframes to produce the Mosquito NF XVII and to the NF XII to become the NF XIX. No 85 Squadron received its first Mosquito NF XVIIs in November and No 25 Squadron began to convert to the new mark in the following month. The Type 21 GCI radar, which was also coming into service, was likewise able to deal with moderate levels of jamming. *Düppel*, the German equivalent of 'Window', duly made its appearance in October, but it was not until the resurgence of Luftwaffe bomber activity in the following January that it was to have any great effect. In November 1943, as preparations for the invasion of Normandy gained momentum, the nightfighter squadrons of Fighter Command were divided. Six of them were earmarked for allocation to the 2nd Tactical Air Force (2nd TAF) which would eventually move to the Continent in support of the Allied armies. The remaining 11 were to be responsible for home defence, within a new command known as Air Defence of Great Britain (ADGB). (The more appropriate title of Fighter Command was re-introduced in October 1944.) Although the six 2nd TAF squadrons would be available for the defence of Britain until mid-1944, it was considered that improvements in the night air defences justified a reduction in forces. By June 1944 the number of fighter sectors in Britain had been reduced to 14, less than half the number operating at the end of 1941.

On the night of 21/22 January 1944 the RAF's defences were once more put to the test, when the Luftwaffe launched Operation 'Steinbock' (known to the British as the 'Baby Blitz'). It was conceived as a series of hard-hitting reprisal attacks, mainly directed against London. Peltz, by that time a Generalleutnant, had at his disposal a force of some 500 nightbombers, which included 46 of the new He177 heavy bombers. It also included a special pathfinder *Gruppe*, I/KG 66, which used the very accurate *Egon* radar blind bombing system. With these resources, it was hoped to emulate the damaging raids which RAF Bomber Command had inflicted on German cities. Heavy jamming with *Düppel* seriously affected the performance of the older GCI equipment and the nightfighters' AI Mk VIII, as had been anticipated. Controllers using Type 21 GCI soon had more contacts than they could handle, but the searchlight co-operation tactics worked well. On the first night of the 'Steinbock' offensive, Fighter Command flew 96 sorties and claimed 16 enemy aircraft destroyed. And, in spite of the Luftwaffe's maximum effort of 447 bomber sorties, much of the bombing went astray. Attacks on London continued until mid-March, after which such targets as Hull, Bristol and various South Coast ports were raided. Losses to the attackers continued to be heavy: by the end of February 129 bombers had been lost and in March and April the loss rate rose to over 8% of sorties flown (150 bombers failing to return during these two months). The German effort had fallen off to such an extent in May — the last month of the offensive — that the loss of some 50 bombers represented a 10% attrition rate.

The defeat of what proved to be the last German-manned bomber offensive against Britain was essentially due to an inexperienced and ill-found bomber force attempting to penetrate strong and effective defences. Much had been expected of *Düppel* jamming, and it certainly reduced the effectiveness of most of Fighter Command's radar equipment. Nonetheless, the newer jam-resistant radars and the searchlights, which relied on sound-location, provided an effective stopgap. Moreover, in order to deal with the speed advantage of the newer German bombers, the RAF Mosquitos had been fitted with the nitrous oxide injection system, which provided a boost in top speed of over 40mph for a period of 6min. The losses inflicted by the British night defences had shattered the morale of the Luftwaffe's bomber crews at a crucial time; the forces assembling in southern England in preparation for the Normandy landings would have provided many vulnerable targets for air attack. As a result, it was not until after the Allied forces had established themselves ashore in France that the Luftwaffe attempted to intervene.

The UK-based nightfighter force had virtually completed its transition from the Beaufighter to the Mosquito by D-Day, the last unit to receive Mosquitos being No 68 Squadron in July 1944. The six Mosquito squadrons of the 2nd TAF (Nos 29, 264, 409, 410, 488 and 604) had primary responsibility for night defence of the beachheads, but their work was supplemented by patrols flown by the ADGB squadrons. On the night of 6-7 June about 150 sorties were mounted by German bombers and for the following five nights their effort was maintained at a level of between 80 and 150 sorties, before dropping to a nightly average of 60 to 70 sorties. In spite of the use of such novel weapons as radio-controlled and glide bombs and the *Mistel* 'pick-a-back' combination (an unmanned explosive-filled Ju88 carried beneath a fighter), comparatively little was achieved by these bombers. By the end of the month 58 bombers had been accounted for by patrolling nightfighters, including two *Mistel* combinations destroyed on the night of 14/15 June by Mosquitos of Nos 410 and 264 Squadrons. The He177 heavy-bombers proved to be especially vulnerable, no fewer than eight of them being destroyed in the week following the landings. By a curious coincidence, all of them were claimed by Mosquitos of No 456 Squadron RAAF, an ADGB unit. One of the successful pilots was Flt Lt R. B. Cowper, who was patrolling north of the Cherbourg peninsula on the night of 9/10 June when he was directed on to a He177; he could see that the aircraft carried glide-bombs outboard of the engine nacelles. Cowper fired three bursts into the bomber, setting its starboard wing alight and he last saw it diving vertically downwards. Immediately afterwards he engaged a Do217, which was likewise destroyed.

The opening of Germany's V-1 offensive against Britain on 13 June immediately diverted resources away from the invasion beachheads. Day- and nightfighters formed London's first line of defence against the flying bombs, with patrols covering an area from the North Downs to mid-Channel. Behind the fighters lay a barrier of AA guns, with the capital's balloon barrage providing a last-ditch defence. As the V-1 had a cruising speed of about 400mph, only the latest dayfighters — Hawker Tempest Vs, Griffon-engined Spitfire XIVs and the first Gloster Meteor I jets — had adequate performance to be reasonably certain of an interception. By night, the Mosquito had barely enough speed to catch a V-1 and so their crews needed to react quickly and accurately if an interception was to be achieved. The first success went to a Mosquito of No 605 Squadron, an Intruder unit, on the night of 14/15 June. Shortly afterwards, four squadrons were assigned solely to anti-'Diver' patrols ('Diver' being the Allied codename for the V-1) and by mid-July nine squadrons were engaged full-time on this work. One advantage enjoyed by the Mosquito crews was that the exhaust flames of the V-1s were very conspicuous by night. Fighters patrolling over the Channel were therefore able to dive down to engage them at a height of some 2,500ft and before they had reached maximum cruising speed. Even

so, good judgement was needed to position the fighter astern of the V-1s and estimation of range was particularly difficult. As there was a considerable danger of friendly fighters in pursuit of the same target colliding, navigation lights would be switched on as the Mosquito dived to attack. The nightfighter then had some 8min in which to complete the V-1's destruction, before it was forced to break away to avoid entering the gun belt.

In mid-July the gun belt was moved forward to the coast, a bold redisposition of forces in the middle of a battle which nonetheless paid dividends. This then created two fighter patrol zones, separated by a gun belt, and the need for fast reaction on the part of the fighters became even more important. Tempests of No 501 Squadron began to operate at night, but the greater part of night patrol work still fell to the Mosquitos. By the time that the V-1 launching sites in France were overrun by the advancing Allied armies, the combined efforts of the defences were accounting for over 70% of V-1s launched. This did not mark the end of the V-1 campaign, though because from July onwards the Luftwaffe had been air-launching these weapons from He111 bombers at night over the North Sea. As the He111s flew at slow speed and low level, they were difficult targets for the Mosquitos. Nevertheless, a total of 77 launch aircraft were lost to all causes, 41 of them on operations of which at least 16 fell to Mosquitos. The V-1 that they carried also became targets for the defences, of course, and only one in 20 of those launched reached their objectives. These attacks ended in January 1945, but the final phase of anti-'Diver' operations were flown in March against long range V-1s launched from Western Holland. The final wartime version of the Mosquito nightfighter, the NF XXX, took part in these patrols. A development of the Mosquito NF XIX, it was powered by Merlin 72 or 76 engines with two-stage superchargers. Fighter Command's first Mosquito NF XXXs entered service with No 25 Squadron in October 1944. Top-scoring nightfighter unit against the V-1s was No 96 Squadron, with 181 destroyed, and its CO, Wg Cdr E. D. Crew, was the most successful Mosquito pilot against these weapons.

The Luftwaffe's operation 'Gisela' brought Fighter Command's Mosquitos into action with the German Intruders, five enemy nightfighters being claimed on 3/4 March 1945. But the focus of night action had shifted to the Continent during the final months of the war. By the end of October 1944 the 2nd TAF's nightfighter squadrons had accounted for 200 enemy aircraft destroyed since D-Day. One of the most successful crews at this time was Flt Lt G. E. Jameson and his navigator Flg Off A. N. Crookes of No 488 Squadron RNZAF. With five victories already to their credit, they had an especially successful patrol off the Normandy coast

Left:
Flt Lt G. E. Jameson (left) and his navigator Flg Off N. Crookes were the most successful Mosquito NF XIII crew of No 488 Squadron, RNZAF. They accounted for eight enemy aircraft destroyed in June and July 1944.
IWM CH13676

on the night of 29/30 July, claiming three Ju88s and a Do217 all confirmed destroyed. The first contact was picked up at 05.02hrs, approaching head-on at 2 miles range. As the sky had begun to lighten, Jameson gained visual contact at 1 mile separation. He identified the aircraft as a Ju88 and Crookes was able to confirm this, using Ross night glasses which had been introduced as an aid to visual identification. Jameson then turned hard to port, coming around astern of the enemy bomber. It then disappeared into cloud, but the target was followed on radar until at 300yd range Jameson again saw it in a gap in the clouds. He fired two short bursts and the Ju88 dived down to crash south of Caen. Shortly afterwards, clouds of *Düppel* alerted Jameson and Crookes to the presence of a second German aircraft. Crookes gained radar

contact and the Mosquito came in astern of a second Ju88 skimming the cloudtops. The enemy bomber attempted evasive action, turning hard to port and diving towards thick cloud. However, Jameson got in a burst of fire before it reached cover and it dived vertically towards the ground. Shortly afterwards a third Ju88 was picked up visually at 4,000yd range. It dived away into cloud, taking violent evasive action and dropping *Düppel*. But, although Jameson was flying a Mosquito NF XIII fitted with AI Mk VIII, radar contact was maintained; he followed the bomber down to just above treetop height, closed in to 250yd range astern and sent the enemy aircraft plunging into the ground. The controller then sent the Mosquito to the northwest, where two radar contacts were picked up. Closing in on the nearest, Jameson

Right:
Wg Cdr F. D. Hughes commanded No 604 Squadron from July 1944 until April 1945. He gained his first night victory on 16 October 1940, when flying Defiants with No 264 Squadron. His last successful combat on 13 January 1945 brought his score up to 18½ enemy aircraft destroyed.
IWM CH14226

identified it as a Do217: it too attempted to shake off the Mosquito in cloud, using violent evasive manoeuvring and releasing large amounts of *Düppel*. But Jameson eventually regained visual contact and shot it down.

During the German Ardennes offensive in December the Mosquito squadrons were in action, despite atrocious weather conditions. By the end of the month they had claimed 28 enemy aircraft destroyed for the loss of one Mosquito. Operations continued over the battlefront into January, with the Allied counteroffensive. On the night of 13/14 January 1945, Wg Cdr F. D. Hughes, CO of No 604 Squadron, was directed by the controller into an interception of a Ju188, 3 miles south of Rotterdam. The bomber was carrying out a gentle corkscrew evasive manoeuvre as the Mosquito

closed in. As Hughes pulled up to fire, he was spotted and the Ju188 began to turn away to port. However, it was too late, as the Mosquito shells hit, setting its starboard engine aflame. The enemy aircraft flicked on to its back and dived vertically into the ground. It was Hughes's final success for the war, bringing his total to 18 and a shared victory. He had fought as a Defiant pilot in the Battle of Britain, shooting down two enemy aircraft, before gaining his first night victory on 15/16 October 1940. By the end of hostilities the 2nd TAF nightfighter squadrons had claimed 299 victories. And, although there were never more than six squadrons flying Mosquito NF XIIIs and NF XXXs, they had provided an effective night defence for the Allied armies during the advance through Western Europe.

6 US Nightfighters 1941-45

Even before the United States entered World War 2, its armed forces were benefiting from the British experience in radar-directed night-fighting. American military observers were able to see at first hand the operations of the RAF's nightfighter squadrons and the GCI stations. And, moreover, the technical secrets of airborne radar were made available to the United States, permitting the establishment of the Radiation Laboratory at the Massachusetts Institute of Technology (MIT) early in 1941. By time of the Pearl Harbor attack, 15 experimental airborne radar sets had been built, based on the RAF's AI Mk IV; and the British scientists' theoretical knowledge of centrimetric radar had been passed on to MIT, allowing it to follow its own lines of development using that principle. In January 1941 the US Army Air Corps (not to become the US Army Air Forces, or USAAF until 20 June 1941) ordered two prototypes of the Northrop XP-61, that service's first specialised nightfighter design. The nightfighter specification had been drawn up by the 'Emmons Board',

chaired by Lt-Gen Delos C. Emmons, Commanding General of GHQ Air Force, who had been one of the officers to visit Britain.

As a result of the British co-operation, work on creating a specialised nightfighter force for the USAAF was well advanced by December 1941. However, even with the benefit of this early start, it was to be September 1942 before a radar-equipped nightfighter reached a frontline squadron. In the meantime, night air defences had to be improved and, since the Hawaiian Air Force Command (which became the 7th Air Force in February 1942) was right in the firing line of the Pacific war, it was that force which took the initiative. The 18th Pursuit

Below:
The Douglas A-20 light bomber provided the basis not only for the RAF's Havoc and Boston nightfighters and Intruders, but also for the USAAF's first nightfighter — the P-70 Night Hawk. The XP-70 prototype was in fact a conversion of the first A-20. McDonnell Douglas

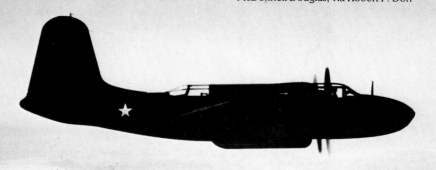

An early-production Douglas P-70 in flight; armament comprised four 20mm cannon carried in a belly-mounted gun pack. The majority of Night Hawks served with training units.
McDonnell Douglas, via Robert F. Dorr

Unit	Date Activated	Aircraft	Air Force	Area of Operations
6th NFS	09.01.43	P-70, P-38, P-61	7th	Central, S and SW Pacific
414th NFS	26.01.43	Beaufighter, P-61	12th	Mediterranean and European Theatres of Operations
415th NFS	10.02.43	Beaufighter, P-61	12th	Mediterranean and European Theatres of Operations
416th NFS	20.02.43	Beaufighter, Mosquito, P-61	12th	Mediterranean and European Theatres of Operations
417th NFS	20.02.43	Beaufighter, P-61	12th	Mediterranean and European Theatres of Operations
418th NFS	01.04.43	P-70, P-38, P-61	5th	SW and W Pacific
419th NFS	01.04.43	P-70, P-38, P-61	13th	S and SW Pacific
420th NFS	01.06.43	P-70, P-61	Remained in USA	No ops
421st NFS	01.05.43	P-70, P-38, P-61	5th	New Guinea, W Pacific Philippines
422nd NFS	01.08.43	P-61	9th	European Theatre of Operations
423rd NFS	01.09.43	P-70	(Redesignated 155th Photo Recce Squadron 22.06.44)	
424th NFS	24.11.43	P-70	Remained in USA	No ops
425th NFS	01.12.43	P-61	9th	European Theatre of Operations
426th NFS	01.01.44	P-61	10th & 14th	China-Burma-India
427th NFS	01.02.44	P-61	10th	China-Burma-India
547th NFS	01.03.44	P-70, P-38, P-61	5th	SW and W Pacific
548th NFS	10.04.44	P-61	7th	W Pacific
549th NFS	01.05.44	P-61	7th	W Pacific
550th NFS	01.06.44	P-61	13th	SW Pacific

USAAF Nightfighter Squadrons 1943-45

Group formed an ad hoc flight of Curtiss P-40Bs and older Curtiss P-36s. They were flown by the more experienced pilots of the Group's six squadrons, each of which provided two aircraft and pilots for night readiness. This arrangement was not satisfactory, though, as a more permanent organisation was required. Accordingly, the night air defence role was assumed as a full-time duty by one squadron, the 6th Pursuit Squadron under the command of Capt Dick Watt. Its specialised role was not formally recognised until 9 January 1943, when the unit was re-designated as the 6th Night Fighter Squadron (NFS). The squadron's P-40s practised night interceptions in co-operation with searchlights and sometimes used information from early-warning radar, although ground-controlled interception techniques were not fully developed until nightfighters with airborne radar became available.

It was apparent that a stopgap, specialised nightfighter would be needed for the USAAF, since the XP-61 did not make its first flight until May 1942 and production deliveries of P-61 Black Widows only began in the summer of the following year. Once more, the USAAF decided to take account of British experience. Just as the RAF had adapted the Douglas DB-7 to the night-fighting and Intruder roles as the Havoc, the USAAF modified the same design (which was in service as the A-20 bomber) to become its first radar-equipped nightfighter.

An initial batch of sixty aircraft, known as the P-70 Nighthawk, was ordered. Carrying a crew of two, it was fitted with SCR-540 radar and armed with four 20mm cannon mounted in a ventral tray. The SCR-540 was the American version of AI Mk IV, which had been put into production by the Western Electric Co. The initial batch of P-70s was delivered to the USAAF between April and September 1942. Further versions of the P-70 were produced by converting A-20 bomber airframes in 1943, but they were intended for use as operational trainers rather than frontline aircraft.

The first unit to become operational on the P-70 was the 6th NFS on Hawaii. Early in 1943 the unit formed two six-aircraft detachments for combat duty, despatching Det A to New Guinea and Det B to Guadalcanal in the Solomons. Both detachments carried out their long trans-Pacific deployment flights, accompanied by two Consolidated LB-30 Liberators. Det B arrived at Henderson Field on Guadalcanal on 28 February 1943 and began patrols in pursuit of 'Washing Machine Charlie', the Japanese night harassment bombers. Both operational and living conditions on the island were very primitive. As there was no integrated command structure for the air defence forces at that time, co-ordination of nightfighter patrols and AA fire was poor and the P-70s often found themselves flying through 'friendly' ack-ack. There were also other handicaps: the SCR-540 radars had the same limitations of range and problems with ground clutter as the British AI Mk IV. But, the biggest worry was that the P-70 had serious performance shortcomings. At heights below 10,000ft, it was found to be relatively fast and manoeuvrable, but at greater altitudes performance fell off rapidly. It took a P-70 over 40min to climb to 20,000ft and attempts to reduce the nightfighter's weight made little difference. The heart of the problem was the P-70's unsupercharged Wright R-2800 Double Cyclone engines, inherited from the A-20. Under these conditions, Det B of the 6th NFS did well to achieve the USAAF's first nightfighter kill, when on 19 April Capt Earl C. Bennett and radar operator Cpl Edwin E. Tomlinson intercepted and shot down a Mitsubishi G4M 'Betty' over Guadalcanal.

Det A's P-70s began operations from '3-Mile Strip', Port Moresby in April 1943. Sporadic night-raiding by Japanese bombers was countered by P-70s held at readiness on the ground, which could be scrambled when radar warned of the approach of enemy aircraft. However, these raids were generally flown at altitudes of 28,000ft and above, which the P-70 were unable to reach. Det A's only success was gained on the night of 19 April, when Lt Burnell W. Adams's radar operator, Flt Off Paul DiLabbio, gained an AI contact below the P-70's patrol height of 26,000ft. Adams closed in to visual range on a Mitsubishi Ki-21 'Sally' and fired a burst of cannon fire, which caused the Japanese bomber to explode in mid-air. Thereafter, the Port Moresby raiders stayed above 28,000ft and the P-70s had no further success. An altitude of 26,000ft was the maximum attainable by Nighthawks which had been modified by the removal of all armour plate, the fitting of paddle-bladed propellers and fuel booster pumps — and at that height the aircraft was barely controllable.

In the summer of 1943, Det B on Guadalcanal obtained a number of Lockheed P-38J Lightnings for night patrol work, relying on searchlight illumination to pick out the Japanese bombers. The P-70s were then relegated to interception work at lower altitudes and Intruder missions over the enemy air bases. By the end of the year the P-38s had accounted for eight Japanese bombers destroyed and, finding that high altitude was no longer a guarantee of immunity, the enemy adopted low-level bombing tactics. The New Guinea detachment was thinking along much the same lines, but its solution to the high-altitude night interception problem was more ambitious. Two P-38Gs were converted into two-seat nightfighters, fitted with SCR-540 radar, but this ingenious design, produced entirely as a field conversion, did not see combat. By the autumn of 1943, the nightfighter training programme in the US was beginning to

US Navy Operational Nightfighter Squadrons 1943-45			
Unit	Aircraft	Carrier/Shore Base	Commanding Officer
VF(N)-33	F6F	USS *Sangamon* USS *Chenango*	Lt-Cdr P. C. Rooney
VF(N)-41	F6F	USS *Independence*	Cdr T. F. Caldwell
VF(N)-53	F6F	USS *Saratoga*	Lt-Cdr A. N. Main
VF(N)-75	F4U-2	Solomon Islands	Lt-Cdr W. J. Wildhelm
VF(N)-76	F6F	Carrier dets	Lt-Cdr E. P. Aurand
VF(N)-77	F6F	Carrier dets	Lt R. M. Freeman
VF(N)-78	F6F	Carrier dets	Cdr J. S. Gray
VF(N)-90	F6F	USS *Enterprise*	Lt-Cdr R. J. McCullough
VF(N)-91	F6F	USS *Bon Homme Richard*	Lt-Cdr A. Minvielle
VF(N)-101	F4U-2	Carrier dets	Lt-Cdr R. E. Harmer

produce results. Training on the P-70 was centred on Orlando Air Base, Florida, until early 1944 when Hammer Field, California, took over this duty. As the crews graduated, they were formed into new nightfighter squadrons for service overseas. The first two such units were the 418th NFS and 419th NFS, which were despatched to New Guinea and Guadalcanal respectively. The 6th NFS detachments were eventually absorbed by these squadrons, although the nucleus of the 6th NFS remained in existence on Hawaii. The personnel of a third nightfighter unit, the 421st NFS, arrived in New Guinea in January 1944 where they were equipped with P-70s and P-38s. By that time the work of night interception was generally carried out by the P-38s, while the P-70s with their good radius of action and

Above:
British-supplied Bristol Beaufighter Mk VI nightfighters were operated by four USAAF nightfighter squadrons in the Mediterranean Theatre of Operations during 1943-45. They usually retained British camouflage and serials, and wore no distinctive unit markings. IWM FRA200680

low-altitude performance concentrated on Intruder and night interdiction missions.

By mid-1944 the Northrop P-61 Black Widow was operational and this aircraft soon superseded the unsuitable P-70 with the front-line units, although the Nighthawk was to remain in service as an operational trainer. The P-61 was a large aircraft, comparable in size and weight with the B-25

Above:
Northrop's P-61 Black Widow was the first American nightfighter to be designed as such from the outset. Some 450 of the P-61B model (illustrated) were built and reintroduced the remotely-operated dorsal turret which had been removed from earlier aircraft because of its unsatisfactory performance. IWM HU3010

medium bomber, and carried a crew of three (pilot, radar operator and gunner). Powered by two Pratt & Whitney R2800 Double Wasp radials, it had a good performance above 25,000ft, good endurance and it was stable and pleasant to fly. Initial pilot reaction to the massive nightfighter was unfavourable, though, and it was unfairly criticised for its sluggish manoeuvrability. Armament comprised four 20mm cannon, plus four 0.5in machine guns in a remotely-operated dorsal turret. The latter feature was often deleted, however, as on the early versions it caused severe buffeting problems and even when retained was usually locked into the fixed, forward-firing position. The nose-mounted radar was the excellent SCR-720 centimetric equipment. First deliveries were made to the 6th NFS in May 1944 and over the next four months the 421st NFS, 418th NFS and 419th NFS converted on to the new nightfighter.

In June 1944 the 6th NFS sent an eight-aircraft detachment to the recently-occupied island of Saipan in the Marianas, gaining their first victories on 6 July when two Mitsubishi G4M 'Betty' bombers were shot down. There followed a lull in operations until the B-29 Superfortresses began to operate from Saipan in October, which provoked a strong Japanese reaction. During three night raids in December, P-61s of the 6th NFS accounted for six G4M 'Bettys'. The most successful pilot was Lt Dale Haberman, who had gained one of the

victories on 6 July. On Christmas night he was ordered to scramble at 20.00hrs and vectored to the north of the island at 15,000ft. Radar operator Lt Raymond Mooney picked up a contact at 5 miles range. Haberman closed in to 500yd range before opening fire: the Japanese bomber began violent evasive turns, but the P-61's shells had found their mark and it dived vertically downwards with a wing on fire. Mooney then told Haberman to turn to starboard, as he had picked up a second contact, 2 miles distant. The P-61 closed in to 200yd behind this bomber, and Haberman's fire caused it to explode in mid-air. The 418th NFS on Mindoro in the Philippines had an even greater success on the night of 29 December. Its CO, Maj Carroll C. Smith, shot down four Japanese aircraft, including a Nakajima Ki-84 'Frank' which was one of the JAAF's best fighters. The P-61s were not generally so effective against Japanese fighters flying at night though. The 421st NFS had to be withdrawn from Leyte and replaced by Hellcat nightfighters of US

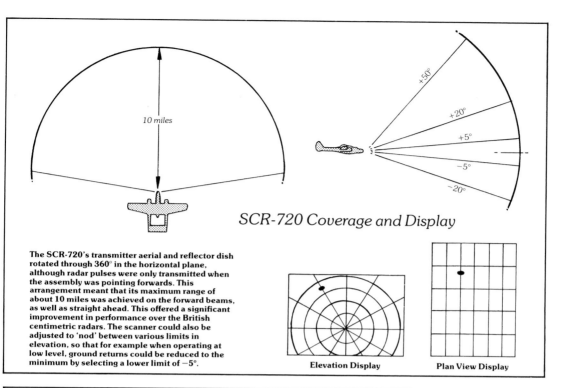

SCR-720 Coverage and Display

The SCR-720's transmitter aerial and reflector dish rotated through 360° in the horizontal plane, although radar pulses were only transmitted when the assembly was pointing forwards. This arrangement meant that its maximum range of about 10 miles was achieved on the forward beams, as well as straight ahead. This offered a significant improvement in performance over the British centimetric radars. The scanner could also be adjusted to 'nod' between various limits in elevation, so that for example when operating at low level, ground returns could be reduced to the minimum by selecting a lower limit of −5°.

Elevation Display   **Plan View Display**

USMC Nightfighter Squadrons 1942-45			
Unit	Aircraft	Date Commissioned	Area of Operations
VMF(N)-531	PV-1	16.11.42	Solomon Islands
VMF(N)-532	F4U-2	01.04.43	Marshall Islands Mariana Islands
VMF(N)-533	F6F	01.10.43	Okinawa
VMF(N)-534	F6F	01.10.43	Mariana Islands
VMF(N)-541	F6F	15.02.44	Palau Islands Philippines
VMF(N)-542	F6F	06.03.44	Okinawa
VMF(N)-543	F6F	15.04.44	Okinawa
VMF(N)-544	F6F	01.05.44	Not operational

Marine Corps squadron VMF(N)-541 on 5 December 1944, because its P-61s were unable to catch the fast night-raiders.

In addition to the original nightfighter squadrons in the Pacific Theatre which converted from the P-70 to the P-61, a further six units were formed with the new nightfighter for service against Japan. The 547th NFS, which had formed at Hammer Field, California on 1 March 1944, began operations in October 1944 with the 5th Air Force. Although its main equipment was the P-61 Black Widow, the squadron also flew P-38 Lightnings.

These were fitted with the APS-4 radar, which had been developed under US Navy contract and were suitable for installation in single-seat fighter aircraft. A small group of selected pilots was given an intensive course of instruction in operating the radar equipment and on 9 November three P-38s and five pilots were detached for duty on Leyte in the Philippines. It was found that the P-38s were not really suitable for night interception duties, but they did provide effective cover in dawn and dusk patrols. The workload of flying the aircraft, operating the radar and then making visual contact

Above:
One of the 419th NFS's Black Widows is seen here on Guadalcanal in 1944. The squadron ended the war based in the Philippines, flying the P-61 until 1946. IWM NYF43956

had proved too great for pilots who had only received the minimum of training in these exacting operational procedures. However, not only were fighting conditions more favourable during the dawn and dusk patrols, but there was also the chance of meeting enemy fighters in daylight. A P-61 would have been fortunate to survive such an encounter, whereas the Lightning could well hold its own. The radar-equipped P-38s also performed well on Intruder missions over enemy airfields. Two days before the P-38 detachment rejoined its parent squadron on Luzon, it gained a shared victory against a Mitsubishi A6M 'Zero' over the town of Lingayen. The experience of the 547th NFS with single-seat P-38s clearly indicated that, while this fighter could certainly make good some of the P-61's performance shortcomings, it was no substitute for the larger fighter on night patrol work.

In March 1945 the 548th NFS and 549th NFS became operational on Iwo Jima with the 7th Air Force. In June 1945 the 548th NFS moved forward to Ie Shima. The 550th NFS had been assigned to the 13th Air Force in December 1944 and began operations over the Philippines in the following month; among the missions flown were night ground-attack sorties. Two nightfighter squadrons served in the China-Burma-India Theatre. The 426th NFS was initially assigned to the 10th Air Force in India in mid-1944, but moved to China during the following October to provide night air defence for the advanced B-29 bases in the Chengtu area. Its first victory was gained on the night of 30 October by Capt Robert R. Scott. By the following spring Japanese nightbomber activities

had all but ceased, and so the squadron went over to Intruder missions. At that time it was joined by P-61s on detachment from the 10th Air Force's 427th NFS, which had been flying Intruder missions over Burma since February.

In the European Theatre of Operations, the greater part of the night-fighting work was carried out by the RAF. However, six USAAF nightfighter units did operate there with the 9th and 12th Air Forces. Four squadrons were trained on the Beaufighter NF Mk VI by the RAF (the 414th, 415th, 416th and 417th NFS), becoming operational in the Mediterranean area during the summer of 1943. One noteworthy operation undertaken by the 414th NFS was the provision of night air cover for the Anzio beachhead in January 1944. On 23 January the squadron's Beaufighters intercepted and shot down a Do217 and a He177 during these patrols. Two P-61-equipped units — the 422nd and 425th NFS — flew with the 9th Air Force. But, although the squadrons' personnel had arrived in Britain by April 1944, their aircraft were slow to follow and operations did not begin until July. From the summer of 1944 onwards, the two units flew in support of the American armies on the Continent, carrying out Intruder sorties as well as defensive patrols. During the German Ardennes offensive they were especially active, with the 422nd NFS claiming 16 enemy aircraft destroyed and earning a Distinguished Unit Citation.

Although the P-61 Black Widow was well established in service by the beginning of 1945, the USAAF decided to order a two-seat, radar-equipped version of the Lightning into service as the P-38M. A total of 75 single-seat P-38Ls were to be modified in this way. The P-38 was fitted with an APS-4 radar and offered improvements in speed, rate of climb, combat range and operational ceiling over the P-61. The radar operator's position was extremely cramped, however, and it was recommended that only men of 5ft 6in height or less be assigned to the aircraft. In the event, the P-38M was too late for combat service in the Pacific. A few examples reached the 418th NFS in Japan during January 1946, but in the following month the programme was abandoned and the existing conversions scrapped. It was generally considered that, notwithstanding its performance advantages, the P-38M was an inferior nightfighter to the P-61.

The US Navy had from the outset championed the concept of the single-seat nightfighter and accordingly had sponsored the development of radars suitable for installation in such aircraft. The Massachusetts Institute of Technology had designed a centimetric radar to this requirement, which was known as AIA (Air Interception Radar Type A). Appearing in late 1942, it weighed only 300lb and the antenna, transmitter and receiver were compactly housed in a pod which could be fitted to the fighter's wing leading-edge; maximum acquisition range was about 5 miles. Both elevation and azimuth information was displayed on the same radar scope, which was mounted on the fighter's instrument panel. Two blips appeared for each target, that on the left indicating its bearing in azimuth, while a second blip on the right indicated whether the contact was above or below and gave some idea of the height separation. It was decided

Below:
This Northrop P-61 is painted with 'Invasion Stripes' at the time of the Normandy landings. By mid-1944 two nightfighter units — the 422nd and 425th NFS — were based in Britain, becoming operational with the 9th Air Force in July.
IWM EA35617

to fit the radar to the Chance Vought F4U Corsair and 32 F4U-1s were modified in this way, being re-designated F4U-2. In order to compensate for the additional weight of the radar equipment, one of the six .5in wing-mounted machine guns was removed and the ammunition load of the remaining guns reduced. Drag from the radar pod, mounted on the starboard wing leading-edge, reduced the Corsair's top speed by about 10kt. Flight testing of the first F4U-2 conversion was completed by the end of January 1943 and in June deliveries began to VF(N)-75, the Navy's first single-seat nightfighter squadron, at Quonset Point Naval Air Station (NAS). This was the home of the Night-Fighter Development Unit, formed on 18 April 1942 to develop and test nightfighter equipment and to

formulate night-fighting tactics. It also became responsible for training the pilots and controllers of the early nightfighter squadrons.

VF(N)-75 deployed to Munda, New Georgia, in September 1943 and began night patrols early in the following month. The F4U-2s early weeks of combat were disappointing, because many interceptions were missed due to late reaction by the fighters, inexperienced ground control and effective evasion tactics by the Japanese bombers, including the use of 'Window'. However, on the night of 31 October/1 November an F4U-2 flown by Lt Hugh D. O'Neill, the squadron's Executive Officer, gained VF(N)-75's — and the US Navy's — first night victory. Operating with US Marine Corps GCI controllers, Maj T. E. Hicks and TSgt Gleason, O'Neill was vectored on to a G4M 'Betty' flying off Vella Lavella and, although he found it difficult to maintain radar and visual contact with the enemy bomber, eventually he sent it down in flames. One of the problems was that the early AIA radar was not attaining its designed maximum range performance and so contacts were generally obtained by the pilot at around 2 miles separation. The high speed of the Corsair then often resulted in the pilot overshooting, as it was difficult to decelerate the fighter quickly. Moreover, inexpert GCI direction during the early interceptions often exacerbated this problem. Eventually, satisfactory tactics were devised, whereby the F4U-2 was brought in astern of its target at a lower level and then slowed down in pulling up to engage. Results immediately improved and during the following weeks the squadron, with only six pilots on strength, claimed five confirmed victories, plus a 'probable'. VF(N)-75 ended its combat tour in the Solomons area during May 1944 and returned to the US.

A second US Navy nightfighter squadron had been formed on the F4U-2 by splitting the original VF(N)-75. The new unit, VF(N)-101, was commissioned in January 1944 and that month a detachment embarked on USS Enterprise as the first carrier-based nightfighters. They were, moreover, the first US Navy F4U Corsairs to operate from a carrier, since early trials had indicated the type's unsuitability for deck landings and all previously commissioned F4U units had consequently been shore-based. The detachment soon discovered that a simple modification to the fighter's undercarriage dealt with the Corsair's deck-landing problems. But a greater difficulty proved to be the reluctance to launch the nightfighters, because of the additional burden that night operations imposed on the carrier's already heavy workload. As a result, the F4U-2's opportunities for combat were limited. Nonetheless good results were obtained during the 7-month combat cruise and 10 night contacts produced claims for five confirmed victories. Two of

Left:
An F6F-5N Hellcat pictured on a sortie from NAS Quonset Point, Rhode Island, in August 1945. That station was the US Navy's centre for the development of nightfighter tactics and training. Note that the Hellcat is armed with two 20mm cannon and four .5in machine guns.
US Navy, via Robert F. Dorr

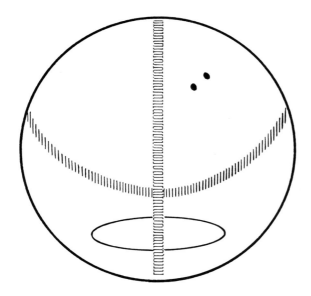

Information from the US Navy's APS-6 radar was presented on a single display for ease of assimilation, since this radar was carried by single-seat fighters. The illustration shows the 'double dot', that on the left being the radar blip; it indicates that the target is to starboard and at about 3 miles range. The 'ghost blip' to the right gives a rough indication of the target's relative altitude — in this case the contact is above. The U-shaped return on the radarscope is the echo from the surface of the sea.

APS-6 Radarscope Display

Below:
A total of 80 radar-equipped F6F-5N Hellcats were supplied to the Fleet Air Arm (FAA), which designated the type Hellcat II NF. Two frontline units including 891 Squadron were equipped with them during 1945. FAA

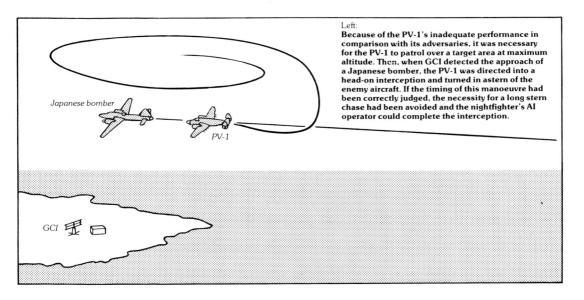

Japanese bomber

PV-1

GCI

USMC PV-1 Interception Tactics

the kills went to VF(N)-101's CO, Lt-Cdr Richard E. Harmer. Equally impressive was the F4U's safety record, since no aircraft were lost during this period, although numerous day missions were flown as well as the night patrols. A second detachment of VF(N)-101 embarked on USS *Intrepid*, but the carrier was damaged in a torpedo attack before the nightfighters had an opportunity to show their mettle. Apart from VF(N)-75 and VF(N)-101, the only other unit to fly the F4U-2 was US Marine Corps squadron VMF(N)-532.

By early 1944 a nightfighter version of the Grumman F6F Hellcat was also in service with the US Navy. This fighter had proved to be equally as adaptable to the night-fighting role as the Corsair and, since it was considered to be a more stable gun platform and much easier to operate from a carrier, it became the standard shipboard nightfighter. At one time it was planned that half of all Hellcats produced should be nightfighters, but in the event shortage of radar equipment prevented this. The initial nightfighter variant of the Hellcat was the F6F-3E, which carried AIA radar. Only 18 of these were built and they equipped VF(N)-76 and VF(N)-77. The developed version of AIA, designated APS-6 was fitted to the F6F-3N version of the Hellcat, 205 of which were produced, and a similar nightfighter conversion of the F6F-5 was designated F6F-5N. One in six of the 6,436 F6F-5s built were the nightfighter version.

The first Hellcat nightfighter missions had in fact been flown by F6F-3 dayfighters of VF-2, operating in co-operation with a radar-equipped Grumman TBF Avenger, during November 1943. The procedure was not a satisfactory one and tragically resulted in the death of Cdr Edward H. 'Butch' O'Hare, the Navy's first ace, on the night of 26 November. Radar-equipped Hellcats became available from early 1944, and by September that year detachments from the two original squadrons, VF(N)-76 and VF(N)-77, and from VF(N)-78 were spread among nine different carriers. The most successful of these was VF(N)-76's Det 2, aboard USS *Hornet*, which claimed a total of 25 victories between April and September 1944. However, significantly, only eight of these had been gained by night. Carrier task group commanders were still reluctant to operate aircraft at night. Lt-Cdr Turner F. Caldwell, CO of VF(N)-79 which had commissioned at Quonset Point on 20 January 1944, believed that the answer to this problem was to form a carrier air group specifically for night operations. He was given the opportunity to prove these theories in August 1944, when Night Air Group 41 embarked under his command aboard USS *Independence*.

As was generally the case with the nightfighter detachments, Night Air Group 41 found that much of its flying was on daylight missions. However, on the night of 12 September 1944, Lt William E. Henry gained the Group's first night victory. He was the leader of a four-aircraft division which was assigned to a dusk combat air patrol. As the Hellcats were returning to *Independence*, the carrier's radar picked up a raider and vectored the nightfighters on to it. Henry picked up a contact on his Hellcat's radar at 7,000yd range and, coming in to close range, he indentified it as a Mitsubishi Ki-46 'Dinah'; his fire caused the Japanese aircraft to blow up in mid-air. Henry, the Executive Officer of VF(N)-41, ended the war as the US Navy's top-scoring nightfighter pilot. He was credited with six enemy aircraft destroyed at night, plus a shared victory, and four day victories. Night Air Group 41 ended its combat tour in January 1941 with 46 enemy aircraft destroyed to its credit. It was relieved by Night Air Group 90 aboard USS *Enterprise*, and in February 1945 a third Night Air Group began operations from USS *Saratoga*. However, this unit (Night Air Group 53) was only in action for five days before *Saratoga* has hit by kamikazes and had to retire. On 14 May 1945, *Enterprise* suffered a similar fate. Thereafter, night air defence of the carrier task forces reverted to the six-aircraft nightfighter detachments.

The US Marine Corps had taken an early interest in the problems of night air defence, seeing it as an indispensable adjunct to their amphibious assault mission. Its first nightfighter squadron, VMF(N)-531, was commissioned at MCAS Cherry Point in November 1942 and it deployed to the South Pacific in September 1943. Its aircraft were Lockheed PV-1 Venturas fitted with SCR-540 radars. The Ventura, which had been originally procured for the Navy as a patrol bomber, was far from ideal as a night-fighter. Like the USAAF's P-70, it lacked the ability to operate at high altitude and, even if the Japanese bombers descended to 15,000ft, it was doubted whether the PV-1s had the speed to overhaul them. In fact, VMF(N)-531 coped very well with the handicaps of unsuitable equipment and inexperience in the new role of radar-directed night-fighting. By the time that its combat tour ended in February 1944, the Venturas had accounted for 12 enemy aircraft destroyed. Significantly, though, all of these combats took place at altitudes between 7.000ft and 15,000ft. The most successful pilots were VMF(N)-531's first CO, Lt-Col Frank H. Schwalbe and his successor Maj John D. Harshberger, each of whom claimed four victories. The Venturas overcame the disadvantages of poor performance by mounting standing patrols, rather than waiting for a radar warning before taking-off; and their controllers usually tried to turn them in astern of a contact from a head-on approach, as this avoided the need for a long stern chase. Although it was VF(N)-75 which gained the first night victory in the Solomons, the controllers of that interception were VMF(N)-531 personnel and the Marine squadron's own first night victory followed two weeks later.

The second US Marine nightfighter squadron, VMF(N)-532, was equipped with the F4U-2 Corsair.

In January 1944 it deployed to Tarawa Atoll in the Gilbert Islands, moving forward to Roi Island and Engebi Island in the Marshalls during the following month. The squadron's first success went to the Corsairs operating from Engebi on 13/14 April. A force of some 12 G4M 'Bettys' was intercepted and Lt Edward A. Sovik and Capt Howard W. Bollman each brought one of the bombers down. A third was probably destroyed by Lt Joel E. Bonner, but his Corsair was hit by return fire and he had to bale out; he was picked up by a destroyer. Lt Donald Spatz was less fortunate; he was misdirected by a controller until out of range and consequently both aircraft and pilot were lost. In June the advanced detachment at Engebi rejoined the rest of the squadron at Roi and in the following month the Corsairs moved to Saipan. However, no further night combats took place before VMF(N)-532 ceased operations and returned to the US in September.

A further five Marine Corps nightfighter squadrons saw action during World War 2, all of them equipped with Hellcats. VMF(N)-541 flew in to Tacloban on Leyte on 3 December 1944, replacing the USAAF's P-61-equipped 421st NFS. The Marine nightfighters gained their first success two nights later, when four Hellcats were flying a pre-dawn patrol over a group of minesweepers. A Nakajima Ki-43 'Oscar' attempted to attack the ships and was sent crashing into the sea by Lt Rodney E. Montgomery. The squadron's early night operations over the Philippines were not entirely satisfactory, however, as the Marine pilots had to work with USAAF GCI controllers who used different procedures. This difficulty was soon overcome, and teamwork much improved, as the two services gained practice in working together. An especially successful combat was fought early on the morning of 12 December, when seven VMF(N)-541 Hellcats intercepted more than 30 Japanese aircraft. Eleven enemy aircraft were destroyed and another damaged for no loss to the Marines. The squadron's deployment to Leyte ended on 6 January 1945 and Gen Douglas MacArthur paid tribute to its magnificent work. During five weeks of combat, it had been credited with 23 enemy aircraft destroyed, five probably destroyed and one Japanese ship sunk and another damaged. But perhaps more remarkably, in flying missions at dawn and dusk and in darkness, from an overcrowded airstrip, often in bad weather, only one aircraft had been lost in an accident and its pilot survived.

The Hellcats of VMF(N)-534 were based on Guam from August 1944 until the end of the war, but the squadron saw little action and its only victory was gained in daylight. However, the invasion of Okinawa in April 1945 provoked a fierce Japanese reaction in the air and three Marine nightfighter squadrons were heavily engaged in the fighting. First ashore were the Hellcats of VMF(N)-542, which landed at Yontan on 7 April. They were followed two days later by VMF(N)-543, operating from Kadena. The two squadrons both gained their first victories on 16/17 April, but, as the dayfighter squadrons battled with the kamikazes, the defence against night nuisance raiders failed to achieve any worthwhile successes. In the first five weeks of the Okinawa campaign, night victories averaged only two per week. The main reason for this poor performance lay with the ground control organisation and especially was due to the bad siting of radar stations to which too little thought had been given in the planning stages of the invasion. Even so, the night defences received a considerable boost on 10 May with the deployment of VMF(N)-533 to Yontan. Commanded by Maj Marion M. Magruder, the squadron had been based in the Marshall Islands since mid-1944. While there it had seen no action, but had taken the opportunity to perfect its skills in night interception. On 15/16 May, Lt Robert M. Wilhide shot down a Mitsubishi G4M 'Betty' for the squadron's first kill. Three nights later the squadron accounted for five Japanese bombers, three of the victories going to Lt Robert Wellwood and the remainder to Lt Edward LeFaivre. Five more victories were added to the squadron scoresheet on 24/25 May and VMF(N)-543 also gained a victory that night. VMF(N)-533's final score of 35 Japanese aircraft was likewise a record. VMF(N)-542 had gained 18 victories during the Okinawa campaign and VMF(N)-543, 15 victories.

As this chapter opened with an account of the way in which Britain helped the US to develop its nightfighter forces, it is appropriate to end with the American contribution to the Fleet Air Arm (FAA) nightfighter programme. As early as 1941, AI Mk IV had been fitted to the Fairey Fulmar, but trials showed no great promise and it was decided to develop the later Fairey Firefly into a carrier-based nightfighter. The Firefly NF II was fitted with AI Mk X radar with transmitter and receiver aerials mounted in separate radomes on the wing leading-edge. It proved to be an ill-conceived arrangement, because synchronisation of transmitter and receiver was difficult to achieve and the pods were mounted too close to the fuselage and propeller, leading to serious interference in signal reception. The Firefly NF II had therefore to be abandoned after only 37 had been built. Fortunately, the American APS-4 ASH radar was available. A remarkably light and compact unit, it had originally been designed for air-to-surface use. However, it worked very well as an AI radar and, as it was fitted in a container pod, it could easily be mounted on virtually any aircraft. The answer to the FAA's nightfighter problem was to fit ASH radar to the Firefly FI dayfighter to produce the Firefly NF I. Eighty Hellcat nightfighters were also supplied to Britain and two FAA squadrons were formed with the type.

Below:
One of the FAA's Fairey Firefly I NF nightfighters, equipped with ASH radar, pictured aboard HMS Ocean. FAA

7 The Jet Nightfighters

Jet nightfighters, although first used operationally by the Luftwaffe during the closing months of World War 2, did not make their appearance in the air forces of the victorious powers until the early 1950s. In the US, the USAAF formed Air Defense Command (ADC) in March 1946 as part of a reorganisation of the service on functional lines. But little serious thought had then been given to the problems of defending the North American Continent from air attack. The US, secure in its monopoly of nuclear weapons, foresaw no threat to its security at that time. However, the Czechoslovak Crisis of 1948 changed the American perception of

Soviet intentions and in the following year the Soviet Union exploded its first A-bomb. The USAF (which had come into being on 18 September 1947) was then forced to consider the possibility of attack on the US by Soviet nuclear bombers. It was a threat which ADC had few resources to meet, and so urgent action was taken to remedy the nation's

Below:
The first Twin Mustang nightfighter was the tenth P-82B 44-65169, which was fitted with SCR-720 radar and redesignated P-82C in 1946.
USAF, via Robert F. Dorr

virtually defenceless state. While interim measures were implemented to provide radar early warning and control in Alaska and the northeastern and northwestern flanks of the US, plans were drawn up for a permanent continental air defence system.

From the outset, the manned interceptor aircraft was seen as the primary air defence weapon and it was realised that the interceptor force must have the capability of operating in all weathers, day or night. In 1945 the only fighter in squadron service with the USAAF which could operate in poor visibility and darkness was the P-61 Black Widow. However, the design was already considered obsolescent and a jet-powered successor, the Curtiss XP-87 Black-hawk, was being developed. Since the XF-87 did not make its first flight until early 1948, an interim replacement for the P-61 was required. (The role prefix 'F' for fighters replaced 'P' for pursuit in 1948.) This was provided by adapting the F-82 Twin Mustang long range escort fighter for the all-weather fighter role. As its name suggests, the Twin Mustang comprised two P-51 Mustang fuselages joined by the wing centre-section and tailplane. The F-82F, G and H all-weather fighter versions carried radar in a pod mounted beneath the wing centre-section and a radar operator replaced the escort fighter's second pilot in the starboard cockpit. A total of 150 all-weather fighter versions was produced, the F-82F coming into service in September 1948. Within two years they had replaced the 116 Black Widows remaining in

the USAF inventory and five fighter (all-weather) squadrons in ADC were flying F-82s by the end of 1949. The type was also deployed overseas with Caribbean Air Command (CAC) and the Far East Air Forces (FEAF).

Although providing a more modern airframe than the wartime vintage P-61 and a better performance, the F-82 was not the ideal aircraft for ADC. It was considered to be hard to manoeuvre and was slow to decelerate. Visibility for the pilot was criticised and it could not operate effectively in poor weather. It did however provide the essential stop-gap between the P-61 and the first jet all-weather fighters. Meanwhile in October 1948 the USAF had re-assessed the possible contenders for its all-weather interceptor fighter requirement. Examining the XF-87 Blackhawk, the Northrop XF-89 Scorpion (originally an all-weather ground-attack fighter) and the Lockheed XF-90 escort fighter, it concluded that the Scorpion would best meet the all-weather fighter requirement. However, it was not particularly enthusiastic about its choice, considering the XF-89 'the best of a poor lot'. A contract for 88 Blackhawks was cancelled and an initial batch of 48 F-89As ordered in their stead.

Anticipating that the F-89's development period would be lengthy, an interim jet all-weather interceptor was ordered at the same time. This aircraft, the Lockheed F-94A Starfire was based on the tried and trusted design of the T-33 jet trainer, with a minimum of modifications to adapt it to the all-weather interceptor role. A version of the trainer's J33 engine with an afterburner was installed, an APG-33 radar fitted in the nose, the rear cockpit was modified to accommodate the radar operator, and four .5in machine guns were carried. A total of 109 F-94As was accepted by the USAF, plus 356 of the essentially similar F-94B variant. The Starfire entered Air Defense Command service in May 1950 and deliveries of F-94A and B models was completed early in 1952. Although lacking in true all-weather capability, the Starfire was considered capable of dealing with the Soviet Tupolev Tu-4 long range bomber (an unlicensed copy of the Boeing B-29 Superfortress). As ADC's first jet all-weather fighter, its performance was a great improvement over that of the F-82. Moreover it inherited the T-33 trainer's pleasant flying characteristics. But perhaps its most noteworthy feature was its Hughes E-1 fire control system (of which the APG-33 radar was part), which enabled an interception and machine gun attack on a bomber to be made entirely 'blind'. Thus by removing the need for visual acquisition of the target — unless this was necessary for identification purposes — the system marked an important milestone in the development of the true all-weather fighter.

The US Navy and Marine Corps nightfighter inventory was strengthened in 1945 by the acquisition of the Grumman F7F-2N Tigercat. This was a twin-engined, two-seat nightfighter, armed

Below:
This 'winterised' nightfighter version of the F4U — the NL variant — was equipped with radar and four 20mm cannon. US Navy via Bruce Robertson

with four 20mm cannon and four .5in machine guns and fitted with an APS-6 radar. It entered service just too late to see combat in World War 2, but it remained in frontline use until 1954. Sixty-six of the F7F-2N version were supplemented by 60 F7F-3Ns and 12 F7F-4Ns, in which the machine gun armament was deleted and an SCR-720 radar replaced the APS-6. Single-seat nightfighters also were kept in service after the introduction of the Tigercat. Forty-eight Grumman F8F Bearcats were built as nightfighters and over 315 of the postwar F4U-5 variant of the Corsair were equipped for this role. However, the Navy was not content to continue flying piston-engined nightfighters and in April 1946 it awarded a contract to Douglas for the design and construction of the turbojet-powered XF3D-1 Skynight. The prototype first flew in February 1950 and the initial production version entered service a year later. Armed with four 20mm cannon, the Skynight had side-by-side seating for pilot and radar operator.

Capt G. G. O'Rourke USN (Ret), who as a lieutenant commanded VC-4's Detachment 44N when its four F3D-2s operated alongside VMF(N)-513 in Korea during June/July 1953, recalled the Skynight:

'It was a grand aircraft in all respects save power. Originally designed for new and powerful Westinghouse J46s, it had to get by with the old, good-but-small J34s that were used in the F2H Banshee series. Its radar system was a true marvel of the era — three distinctly different sets, four scopes, two massive antennas forward (one within the other) and one aft. The APS-21 did the searching with its 30in dish, the APS-26 was the lock-on set, feeding a gun-laying computer and

Below:
A Marine Corps F4U-4B Corsair of VMF-214 'The Black Sheep' is prepared for a night interdiction mission over Korea from USS *Sicily* in September 1950. US Navy, via Robert F. Dorr

presenting both a complicated tracking picture for the RIO (radar interceptor operator) and a super-simple "collapsing circle/dot" picture for the pilot. The APS-28 was a totally self-contained tail warning set that covered a 70° arc in all quadrants astern, presenting both a double-dot scope and four tail warning lights in the cockpit, and with adjustable range coverage and adjustable light sensitivity. We used four miles in combat and thought so much of the 28 that we would not cross the 38th Parallel without it in apple-pie order, which it usually was. We would, also, *not* fly the F3D in daylight, when it would be a sitting duck for a MiG-15 and we were very apprehensive and cautious about bright moonlight flying, when we would seek out and hide in any available cloud.'

It was at this point in the history of postwar nightfighter development that the outbreak of the Korean War (in June 1950) provided an opportunity to test these aircraft in combat — albeit on a limited scale. The three F-82-equipped units of the FEAF, the 4th, 68th and 339th Fighter (All-Weather) Squadrons, were initially used as long range escort fighters in daylight. The latter two units were providing air cover over Seoul on 27 June when North Korean fighters appeared and in the ensuing dogfight the F-82s shot down three of them for the first air victories of the war. In the following month a three-aircraft flight of the 68th Fighter (All-Weather) Squadron began long range night interdiction missions over Korea. However, the F-82's efforts were limited by spares shortages and they were only considered for use in attacking fixed targets. On the night of 30 August two F-82s on a night mission to railway marshalling yards near Seoul destroyed three locomotives and some rolling stock. The Twin Mustang remained in service until early 1952 with the 68th Squadron. But with the aircraft nearing the end of its service life, intensive operations were out of the question and the greater part of the night effort during the early part of the Korean War fell to the US Marine Corps nightfighter squadrons.

Two Marine squadrons, VMF(N)-513 and VMF(N)-542, were operating over Korea during the summer of 1950. However, in February 1951

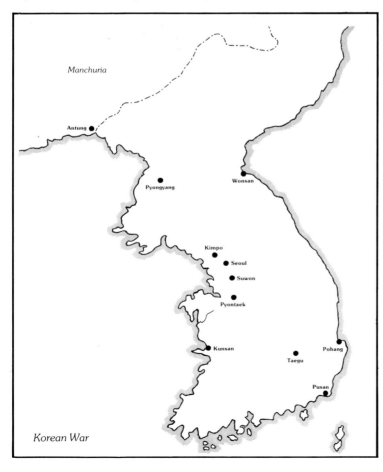

Manchuria

Antung

Pyongyang

Wonsan

Kimpo

Seoul

Suwon

Pyontaek

Kunsan

Taegu

Pohang

Pusan

Korean War

Right:
Grumman F7F-3N Tigercats of VMF(N)-513 'The Flying Nightmares' carried out numerous night interdiction missions over Korea and accounted for two Po-2 'Bedcheck Charlies' destroyed during defensive patrols.
US Marine Corps,
via Robert F. Dorr

VMF(N)-542 returned to the US and VMF(N)-513, which took over the former unit's F7F Tigercats, was left as the only Marine nightfighter unit in combat. Its equipment at that time was a mix of F4U-5NL Corsairs and F7F-3N Tigercats. Their primary role was interdiction behind the battlefront, operating in co-operation with flare-dropping aircraft to attack North Korean truck convoys. But in December 1950 during the 1st Marine Division's breakout from the Chosin Reservoir where they had been encircled by Chinese Communist troops, the Corsairs and Tigercats of VMF(N)-513 and VMF(N)-542 flew night close-support missions. By mid-1951 VMF(N)-513, operating from K-1 airstrip, Pusan, was flying 18 missions each night, this effort representing over 50% of all American night tactical sorties at that time. Many of the squadron's pilots were highly experienced in night operations and Capt Robert Baird, the only Marine Corps nightfighter ace of World War 2, flew with the squadron. In a three-month period between 1 April and 30 June 1951 the squadron carried out 11,980 attacks on enemy vehicles and claimed 1,420 of them destroyed.

In June 1951 the North Koreans began to fly night harassment missions against United Nations forces, using Polikarpov Po-2 biplane trainers in much the same way as the Soviet Air Force had employed them during World War 2. This new development in the air war gave VMF(N)-513, 'The Flying Nightmares', the opportunity to revert to the night interception work which was their primary mission. However, the slow-flying and manoeuvrable Po-2s (known to the Americans as 'Bedcheck

Charlies') were difficult targets for the nightfighters to intercept and their wood and fabric airframes made them poor radar targets. Sometimes the nightfighters were close to ramming the elusive biplanes, but still were unable to pick them out from the ground clutter on their radarscopes. The Po-2s invariably flew at low level, making use of terrain masking to cover their approach from ground radars. The first Po-2 kill went not to a nightfighter but to a Douglas B-26 Invader of the 8th Bomb Squadron flown by Capt Dick Heyman. Then on the night of 30 June, Capt Edwin B. Long, flying a Tigercat with radar operator WO Robert C. Buckingham, intercepted one of the elusive Po-2s 14 miles north of Kimpo airfield. Buckingham picked up the contact on his radar and directed Long into a visual interception on a Po-2 flying at about 80kt. Because of its slow speed, Long was unable to position the Tigercat astern of his target, but visibility was good enough to allow him to attack from a diving pass. His fire was returned, apparently from a sub-machine gun carried by the North Korean observer, but without effect. However, on the third run, the Tigercat's 20mm shells found their mark and the Po-2 crashed to the ground in flames.

'The Flying Nightmares' next success went to a Corsair flown by Capt Donald Fenton, who shot down a Po-2 on 12 July. There followed a lull in North Korean night harassment raids until mid-September. On the night of 23 September the tactical air direction centre at Seoul, call-sign

'Dentist', picked up a Po-2 as it carried out an attack on Kimpo airfield. Two small bombs were dropped, damaging two F-86 Sabres. As the airfield's 20mm automatic AA guns had failed to hit the raider, 'Dentist' scrambled an F7F Tigercat flown by Maj Eugene Van Grundy, with radar operator MSgt T. H. Ullom. The Tigercat caught up with the 'Bedcheck Charlie' north of Seoul and shot it down. In addition to the Corsairs and Tigercats of VMF(N)-513, night air defence of the South Korean capital was provided by two F-82 Twin Mustangs, detached from their base at Itazuke in Japan to stand night alert on one of the Seoul area airfields. Another expedient for dealing with the 'Bedcheck Charlies' was the arming of four North American T-6 Texan trainers (widely employed in Korea as forward air control aircraft, using the radio call-sign 'Mosquito'). This quartet was kept on night alert at Kimpo.

In December 1951 high-flying MiG-15s were detected carrying out sweeps over Seoul at night and, while the current night defences were adequate to deal with Po-2s, clearly they could do

Below:
The Douglas F3D-2 Skynight was the most successful nightfighter type of the Korean War and was responsible for the first jet-versus-jet nightfighter victory in the history of air warfare. VMF(N)-513 began to operate the type during the late summer of 1952.
US Marine Corps, via Robert F. Dorr

nothing against the Communist jet fighters. Accordingly it was decided to deploy jet night-fighters to South Korea as a matter of urgency. The 68th Squadron at Itazuke accelerated its conversion on to the F-94B Starfire and from December onwards detached two of the jet nightfighters to Suwon in South Korea for local night air defence. In addition, ADC's 319th Fighter-Interceptor Squadron, which flew F-94Bs from McChord AFB, Washington, was alerted for overseas service and it deployed to Suwon in March 1952. However, as the threat of further night incursions by the MiG-15s did not materialise, the F-94Bs saw no action. As their E-1 fire control system was still secret equipment, the Starfires could not be risked on operations over enemy territory and so for most of 1952 they were restricted to carrying out local air defence scrambles under strict ground radar control. Ironically the only night victory at this time went to a piston-engined F4U-5NL Corsair of VMF(N)-513, when Lt John W. Andre shot down a Yak-9 on 7 June 1952.

During the summer of 1952 VMF(N)-513 took on the new role of flying night escort missions to the B-29 bombers over North Korea. Darkness was no longer providing adequate cover for their operations and Communist fighters operating under GCI control but with no AI radar, had scored a number of successes by making use of flare illumination or moonlight. Four F7F Tigercats were made available for bomber support missions each night, sweeping the target area about 5min ahead of the bombers. However, they lacked the performance to take on the MiG-15 jets and so VMF(N)-513's re-equipment with F3D-2 Skynight jets went ahead as a matter of urgency. The new fighters were able to fly barrier patrols 20 to 50 miles to the north of the bombers, with the aim of cutting off any enemy fighters which attempted to intercept. 'The Flying Nightmares' first successful combat on a bomber support mission came on the night of 3 November. The Skynight flown by Maj William T. Stratton, with radar operator Hans C. Hoglind, was vectored by ground control on to a contact near Sinuiju. Hoglind brought Stratton in astern of a single-engined jet, which was identified as a Yak-15. Stratton fired three bursts of cannon fire into the enemy aircraft and saw hits on the wing and fuselage. It then exploded and fell away. This was the first jet nightfighter victory by American forces. A second followed within a week, for on the night of 8 November, Capt Oliver R. Davis and radar operator WO F. Fessler shot down a MiG-15.

The Skynights were joined on bomber support patrols by the 319th FIS's F-94B Starfire in November, when the USAF Chief of Staff Gen Hoyt S. Vandenberg personally sanctioned their use over North Korea. The suspected use of decoy tactics by the enemy led to a change in bomber support procedures in January 1953. It was believed that while one group of North Korean fighters lured away the nightfighter covering force, a second group was orbiting high above, ready to come down and attack the bombers once their escorts had been drawn off. This strategem was countered by diverting the Skynights from their barrier patrols to provide overhead cover for the B-29s. Flights of F3D-2s flew at heights of 2,000ft to 3,000ft above the Superfortresses during their run in from the initial point to bomb release over the target. They were then in a position to intervene should the bombers come under fighter attack. Meanwhile, four to six F-94Bs set up a barrier patrol 30 miles ahead of the target. The 319th FIS commander, Lt-Col Jack C. West, reported that the enemy fighters usually turned tail, rather than attempting to penetrate the screen of F-94Bs. This of course achieved the objective desired, although it was frustrating for the USAF nightfighter pilots who were anxious to score the squadron's first victory.

However, it was the Marine pilots who saw most of the action in January 1953, which suggests that the Americans' reading of the enemy's tactics was absolutely correct. VMF(N)-513 accounted for three MiG-15s destroyed during the month. The first combat was fought on the night of 12 January by Maj Jack Dunn and radar operator MSgt Lawrence J. Fortin. Contact was gained as the enemy fighter approached the target area, but then the MiG-15 dropped down below 3,000ft and disappeared from Fortin's radarscope. It was not until the B-29s had released their bomb-loads and withdrawn that the MiG was picked up again. It took Dunn 5min to get on to the enemy fighter's tail, as it was carrying out a series of figure-of-eight turns. He then fired six short bursts of cannon fire, but the MiG escaped apparently unscathed and began to climb away from the Skynight. This gave Dunn the opportunity for another attack, which was much more effective. The MiG caught fire and dived straight for the ground. The second victory went to Capt James R. Weaver and MSgt Robert P. Becker on 28 January. Three nights later Lt-Col Robert F. Conley — who had only recently taken command of 'The Flying Nightmares' — was flying an escort mission, when his radar operator MSgt James N. Scott picked up a contact. Conley closed in below and astern of a MiG-15, which he saw silhouetted against the moon before his fire sent it plunging down to crash into snow-covered mountains.

It was on the same night that the 319th FIS gained its first victory. Ironically the successful crew, Capt Ben L. Fithian and radar operator Lt Sam R. Lyons, were assigned to alert duty at Suwan that night. They were scrambled to escort in an F-80 with a defective air speed indicator and then sent north to replace a Starfire on barrier patrol which was experiencing trouble with its radar. While en route to its patrol station, Fithian's Starfire was vectored on to an enemy aircraft flying at 5,000ft to the west of Pyongyang. Lyons picked it up on radar at 5 miles range. Fithian dropped down to low level, so that he could attack the lower-flying enemy aircraft (believed to be a Lavochkin La-9) in a climb and so avoid the danger of overshooting. Having gained a radar 'lock-on', Fithian opened fire using the E-1's automatic, radar-directed firing mode as he had not yet picked up his target visually. The first two bursts apparently missed, so Fithian eased the control stick from side-to-side, spraying his third burst over a wider area. He immediately saw the impact of his armour-piercing incendiary rounds and, concentrating his fire on that point, saw the enemy aircraft catch fire. He watched it go down to crash before he was vectored on to a second contact. But, the F-94B was by then low on fuel and, on running into intense ground fire, Fithian decided to break-off and return to base.

Meanwhile in October 1952 the 'Bedcheck Charlie' raids had resumed, creating considerable problems for the jet nightfighters. On 13 October four Po-2s bombed and strafed a radar station on the island of Cho-do. An F-94B attempted to intercept and on six occasions gained a radar contact on one of the biplanes, but each time the Po-2 escaped by violent evasive manoeuvres. The only success gained that winter went to a Marine Skynight flown by Lt Joseph A. Corvi and radar operator MSgt Dan R. George on 10 December. Operating in pitch darkness and so unable to make use of the usual, elusive contour-hugging tactics, the Po-2 was picked up by ground radar and the Skynight was directed into radar range. Closing astern to minimum range, the F3D-2's radar was locked-on, but Corvi was unable to acquire the target visually. He therefore opened fire, using the radar information projected on to his gunsight. Fragments of the hapless Po-2 then showered past the Skynight. Corvi was immediately vectored on to a second contact and again getting a radar lock-on — but no sight of the enemy aircraft — fired using radar sighting. No effects were seen from this attack, although the contact faded from the radar screens, and so Corvi and George could only be awarded a probable victory from their second combat.

There was a lull in the 'Bedcheck Charlie' attacks for the first three months of 1953, but when they resumed in mid-April the North Korean pilots were careful to keep to low altitudes where they would be lost in the ground clutter on the nightfighters' radarscopes. An F-94B gained one success on the early morning of 3 May — but at an unacceptable price. Lt Stanton G. Wilcox, with radar operator Lt Irwin L. Goldberg, throttled back his Starfire to a speed of 110mph to get behind a low-flying Po-2 — the 319th FIS crew got their victory, but immediately afterwards the F-94B stalled and

crashed into the ground killing both crewmembers. Similarly, when the 319th FIS commander Lt-Col Robert V. McHale tried to get into an attacking position behind a Po-2 on the night of 12 June, he miscalculated and collided with it. Both McHale and his radar operator Capt Samuel Hoster were killed. And on 16/17 June a raiding force of 15 Po-2s, La-11s and Yak-18s started fires at Inchon which resulted in the loss of 5 million gallons of fuel. It was apparent that the F-94Bs were totally unsuited to operations against the 'Bedcheck Charlies'. In all, four enemy aircraft were claimed as destroyed by the Starfires, while 28 F-94s were lost during the same period, mostly in accidents. Yet, in general, the aircraft proved to be both rugged and reliable, often operating in weather which grounded most other machines.

Piston-engined nightfighters rather than jets offered the best opportunities of engaging the enemy night nuisance raids and so the 5th Air Force requested the loan of four F4U-5N Corsairs from the US Navy's Task Force 77. These radar-equipped fighters had been carrying out night attack missions, Composite Squadron Three (VC-3) providing detachments of F4U-5Ns for the TF77 carriers. Armed with four 20mm cannon and carrying the APS-19A radar with a range of about 3½ miles, the F4U-5N was well suited to the job of hunting down the 'Bedcheck Charlies'. Lt Guy P. Bordelon from the USS Princetown VC-3 detachment brought down five of the raiders in just two months, to become the undisputed 'Bedcheck Charlie' ace — and incidentally the only US Navy ace of the Korean War. On 30 June, the third night of operations by the F4U-5Ns, Bordelon was vectored on to a radar contact. The enemy aircraft was flying at speeds of only 80 to 130kt and carrying out a series of evasive manoeuvres, so that it took Bordelon over half-an-hour to convert his radar contact into a sighting. He was able to decelerate sufficiently by the use of flaps to get into a firing position and his opening burst sent the enemy aircraft (identified as a Yak-18) down to crash into the sea. He then went through much the same procedure to shoot down a second Yak-18. Another two North Korean raiders — on this occasion La-11s — were shot down by Bordelon shortly before midnight on 1 July, and his fifth and final victory, another Yak-18, was gained on the night of 16 July.

The war in Korea had emphasised the importance of strong air defences for the US homeland. The beginnings of an effective all-weather interceptor force came into being in the early 1950s, with the entry into service of the early model F-89 Scorpions and the F-94C variant of the Starfire. The increase in international tension occasioned by the Korean War led to the strengthening of ADC by the recall of reservists and the assignment of ANG squadrons to active duty. In the spring of 1953 the permanent radar system replaced the earlier improvised air defence radar network and a Ground Observer Corps provided the information on low level attack which radar was unable to furnish. Air defence identification zones were established around the nation's borders, in which all movements had to be accounted for or investigated as potentially hostile. With the co-operation of the Federal Aviation Authority and the Military Air Transport Service, flight plans were received and correlated for all friendly aircraft movements and any radar contacts which could not be so identified were then investigated. Thus the new generation of all-weather interceptors had the back-up of a well planned command and control system on the ground.

The F-94C Starfire which came into service with the 437th FIS at Otis AFB, Massachusetts in March 1953 differed in a number of important respects from the earlier F-94A and B versions. It had been fairly extensively redesigned and re-engined with the Pratt & Whitney J48-P-5 turbojet, which developed 8,300lb thrust with afterburning. This gave a maximum speed at sea level of 556kt — 30kt more than the F-94A's maximum speed. And the improvement in rate of climb was even more marked — that for the F-94A being 4,250ft/min, while the F-94C's was 7,980ft/min. But the most important changes were in avionics and armament:

the E-5 fire control system replaced the E-1 and the machine guns gave way to a battery of 48×2.75in, unguided FFAR (folding fin aerial rockets). A total of 387 F-94Cs was built, but reliability was initially poor. The most serious problem was that when the nose load of 24 rockets were fired (the remaining 24 FFARs were in wing-mounted pods), it invariably resulted in an engine flameout. A refinement of the E-5 fire control system was that the autopilot could be coupled in to give automatic steering on to the target once the radar had been locked-on. However, in practice this usually gave the crew too rough a ride, with high 'g' forces and rapid roll rates being generated by the automatic system. Most pilots therefore preferred to fly a manually-steered attack. Rocket-firing was usually done automatically, though with a computer calculating the optimum firing point using inputs from the radar. For all its advanced features — or in truth because so many of them were insufficiently developed — the F-94C was not a successful all-weather interceptor. Yet, such were the problems in finding

Below:
Northrop's F-89D Scorpion first entered Air Defense Command (ADC) service in January 1954 with the 18th Fighter-Interceptor Squadron (FIS) based at Minneapolis-St Paul, Minnesota. It was the most numerous of the Scorpion variants.
US Air Force, via Robert F. Dorr

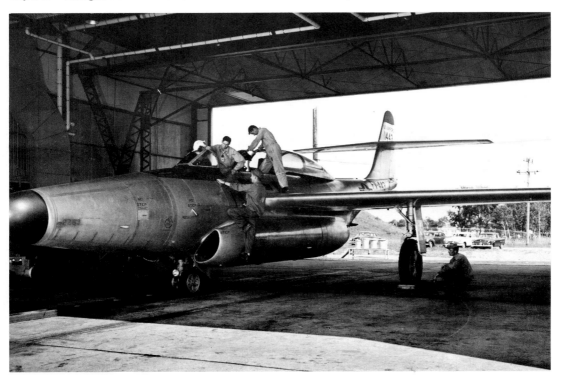

a satisfactory successor, that it remained in frontline service with Air Defense Command until early 1959.

As the USAF had anticipated from the outset, the development of the F-89 Scorpion all-weather interceptor was a protracted process and the basic aircraft went through six different variants during less than a decade of service with the active duty fighter interceptor squadrons. A total of 211 of the cannon-armed F-89A, B and C versions were built before they were supplanted in production by the D model with an all-FFAR armament. These early versions suffered numerous problems with the General Electric J35 turbojets, and their development period had been so long that they were virtually obsolescent before coming into service. Many of these troubles had been cured with the F-89D, but the fighter nonetheless suffered from structural limitations which restricted its high-altitude performance. Thus, while providing an adequate defence against the ageing Tu-4, it was not able to deal with the latest Tu-20 'Bear' or M4

'Bison' Soviet strategic bombers. But a significant improvement in weaponry promised to go some way towards redressing the balance, for the F-89H Scorpion was armed with the Hughes GAR-1 Falcon air-to-air missile, six of which were carried in wingtip pods. The improved E-9 fire control system replaced the earlier F-89's E-6 equipment. Once again development difficulties delayed this model's introduction into service and for that reason its operational life was comparatively short. The first F-89Hs were delivered to the 445th FIS in March 1956, but by the end of the decade the type had disappeared from the frontline inventory. Another weapon which improved ADC's prospects of dealing with the latest generation of Soviet bombers was the AIR-2A Genie rocket. Armed with a low-yield nuclear warhead, this fearsome weapon could be fired in a 'snap-up' attack at bombers flying at a higher altitude than the interceptor. A total of 350 F-89Ds were modified for this armament, being redesignated F-89J. They first entered service in January 1957.

Notwithstanding its problems in acquiring a

North American Air Defence 1956

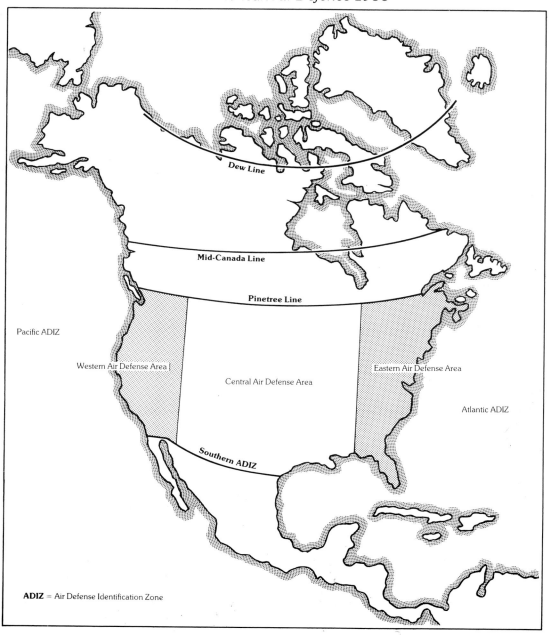

Dew Line

Mid-Canada Line

Pinetree Line

Pacific ADIZ

Western Air Defense Area

Central Air Defense Area

Eastern Air Defense Area

Atlantic ADIZ

Southern ADIZ

ADIZ = Air Defense Identification Zone

satisfactory all-weather interceptor, ADC had grown in strength to an impressive degree by the mid-1950s. There were 55 fighter interceptor squadrons equipped with all-weather aircraft under its control by the end of 1954. Gun and unguided rockets were about to be supplemented by air-to-air missile armament. An important increase to the Command's fighter strength had been made possible by the adaptation of the F-86 Sabre dayfighter for the all-weather mission. Basically the conversion involved the fitting of a nose-mounted

Right and below:
Armament of the F-86D comprised 24 'Mighty Mouse' 2.75in rockets carried in a retractable ventral tray. They were automatically salvoed at the target during a head-on pass, on command from the fighter's Hughes E-4 fire control system.
USAF, via Maurice Allward

radar as part of the E-3 (later E-4) fire control system and a retractable ventral tray housing 24 'Mighty Mouse' 2.75in rockets. The resultant F-86D entered service in the spring of 1953 and by the end of the year 600 fighters of this type were in service. Thereafter the build-up was even more rapid, for in mid-1955 over 70% of the 1,405 interceptors in ADC's inventory were F-86Ds. The USAF finally accepted 2,504 F-86Ds, 981 of which were converted to F-86L configuration. The principal change in this model was the fitting of a data link, which enabled the receipt of information from the SAGE (semi-automatic ground environment) system. SAGE marked the peak of ground radar and control centre development in the 1950s, being a computerised command and control system

Top:
An F-86D salvoes its 'Mighty Mouse' rockets; the deployment of these weapons' folding fins can be seen clearly in this photograph. Maurice Allward

Above:
The Convair F-102A Delta Dagger succeeded the all-weather Sabre in ADC during the late 1950s and by 1958 F-102s made up half of the Command's interceptor inventory. General Dynamics

which could monitor the entire air defence battle. By the late 1950s there had been tremendous progress in radar systems, with the DEW (distant early warning) Line in operation in the far north, backed up by the Mid-Canada and Pinetrees Lines;

Top:
One of the 27th FIS's F-102As lifts off on a murky winter's day. The squadron received Delta Daggers in 1957 at Griffis AFB, New York and relinquished them in favour of the F-106A in 1960. Robert F. Dorr

Above:
F-102As of the 482nd FIS stand on 15min alert at Homestead AFB, Florida, during the Cuban Missile Crisis of 1962. USAF, via Robert F. Dorr

and the seaward flanks were surveyed by radar picket ships, Texas Towers (offshore platforms mounting radar stations) and the first airborne early warning aircraft.

Throughout the vicissitudes of all-weather fighter development, ADC kept its sights on requirements for the 'ultimate interceptor', which was first formulated in 1950. Essentially, this aircraft would combine the traditional nightfighter's all-weather combat capability with the performance of the single-seat dayfighter. The Convair F-102A Delta

Dart owed its inception to this ambitious objective, but in reality it proved to be none other than a more capable successor to the F-86D/L Sabre. Having a supersonic performance, the F-102A was armed with a combination of 2.75in FFARs and Falcon guided missiles; the latter included the nuclear-armed AIM-26 Falcon. Its E-9 fire control system was an improved version of the E-4 fitted to the Sabre. Later modifications included the deletion of the unguided rocket armament, the replacement of the E-9 with the MG-10 fire control system and the provision of an infra-red search and tracking system for low level target detection. The F-102A entered service with the 327th FIS at George AFB, Ca, in April 1956. By the end of 1958 there were 627 F-102As in service with ADC, replacing the F-86D as its most numerous aircraft type. In all, 875 of the total of 889 F-102As accepted by the USAF were assigned to frontline units; a two-seat conversion trainer, the TF-102A was also produced. F-102As were deployed to South-East Asia in small numbers between 1962 and 1969, but saw no combat. By

1969 most of ADC's F-102As had been passed on to the Air National Guard (ANG), which then had over 300 in service. Twenty-three ANG fighter interceptor squadrons were equipped with F-102As.

The US Navy's fighter development programme in the 1950s aimed to produce a single-seat shipboard fighter with limited all-weather capability. The Vought F7U-3 Cutlass, which entered service in 1954, was a cannon-armed interceptor. Sufficient numbers were built to equip only four squadrons. However, the F7U-3M version was significant as it was modified to carry four Sparrow I beam-riding air-to-air missiles. The McDonnell F3H-2 Demon of 1956 was a more capable all-weather interceptor, which in its F3H-2M version was armed with the semi-active radar-homing Sparrow III (AIM-7C). The Douglas F4D-1 Skyray, which was a contemporary of the Demon, also had an all-weather capability but carried only cannon armament, while the F-8D version of the Crusader also had a limited all-weather capability combined with short range

cannon and AIM-9 Sidewinder AAM armament. Without doubt though the US Navy's most important contribution to the development of all-weather combat capability was its introduction of the AIM-7 Sparrow AAM in 1958. This medium range missile — which for the first time permitted the engagement of targets beyond visual range — was operationally deployed with F3H-2Ms during the Lebanon and Quemoy crises of 1958.

Britain, which had done so much of the pioneering work in night-fighting, lagged behind the US in postwar all-weather fighter development.

The UK's night air defences in 1946 depended upon six squadrons equipped with the Mosquito NF 36, the ultimate version of the nightfighter Mosquito which remained in service until 1953. However, the problems of defending a comparatively small island from nuclear-armed jet bombers clearly demanded something better. The first generation of jet nightfighters — Gloster Meteor NF11s, 12s and 14s, de Havilland Vampire NF10 and Venom NF2s and 3s — offered little improvement. On exercises they were frequently outperformed by the RAF's Canberra jet bombers, and were unlikely to have performed any better against the latest Soviet aircraft (the Ilyushin Il-28 was broadly comparable in performance to the Canberra). It was realised that the key to the successful defence of the UK lay in early interception way out to sea, and that could only be achieved through improved warning times and better interceptor performance. Moreover, it was already clear that the hitherto separate problems of day and night

Top:
The Fleet Air Arm's de Havilland Sea Hornet NF 21 nightfighter carried ASH radar in a nose radome and was armed with four 20mm cannon. The only frontline unit to fly the type was 809 Squadron, which operated it from January 1949 to May 1954.
FAA

Above:
No 46 Squadron became the first RAF unit to fly the Gloster Javelin in March 1956. The F(AW)1s illustrated were equipped with 30mm cannon, but later marks carried Firestreak air-to-air missiles. Fighter Command replaced the two-seat Javelin with the single-seat Lightning.
Gloster via Bruce Robertson

defence would better be tackled by an all-weather fighter capable of operating by day or night. The Gloster Javelin, which entered service in 1956, was armed in its later versions with the Firestreak infra-red homing missile. Yet, it was a heavy two-seat fighter which did not approach its contemporary dayfighters in performance. An important innovation in ground control in the mid-1950s did improve the reaction time of the air defences, though: this was the introduction of master radar stations, which combined the functions of the early warning and GCI stations with sector operations. Thus the same unit which received early warning of attack became responsible for scrambling fighters to meet it and directing the subsequent interception.

The Soviet Union, threatened by the might of the USAF's Strategic Air Command, also gave much thought to the problems of air defence in the postwar years. Indeed its air defence forces,

PVO-Strany, emerged in 1954 as a separate service independent of the air force. Initially, its night interception capability was very limited. MiG-15s operating over North Korea had no air interception radar, but had to rely on searchlight or flare illumination for target acquisition. But, in 1955 a limited all-weather capability was provided by the MiG-17PF, fitted with Izumrud AI radar; the MiG-19 was also modified in that way. In 1953 the Soviet Union had flown the prototype of its first true all-weather jet fighter, the Yak-25, and some 600 of these were built over the following four years. However, by the end of the decade the Soviet Union still lacked a fully effective all-weather fighter force; nor had it at that time a comprehensive command and control system.

Above:
The de Havilland Sea Venom F(AW) 21, which succeeded the Sea Hornet NF 21 in 1954, was a 'navalised' version of the RAF's Venom NF 2. WM542, a Mk 20 of 809 Squadron, is pictured. FAA

Left:
Gloster Meteor NF12 WS719 served with No 25 Squadron at West Malling and Tangmere before she was eventually scrapped in March 1959. Bruce Robertson Collection

Below left:
Armed with Firestreak air-to-air missiles and unguided 2in rockets — 28 of which were stowed internally — the de Havilland Sea Vixen F(AW) 1 entered FAA service in 1959 and served with four frontline units. FAA

133

8 The Modern Interceptor

By the end of the 1950s the specialised nightfighter — or all-weather interceptor as it had become known — had reached its ultimate stage of development. From then onwards the hitherto separate design streams of dayfighter and nightfighter merged to produce the modern interceptor which can operate at will both by day and night.

The USAF's 'Ultimate Interceptor', the Convair F-106A Delta Dart, entered service in the spring of 1959. It was designed to an ambitious requirement which called for a fighter which would be capable of intercepting and destroying enemy aircraft under all weather conditions and 'under automatic guidance provided by the ground environment and the aircraft's fire control system'. Carrying guided missiles and nuclear-armed rockets, the F-106 was to have a maximum speed of Mach 2, an operating radius of 375nm and a service ceiling of 70,000ft.

Initially, ADC (which was to be retitled Aerospace Defense Command in January 1968) envisaged an interceptor force of 40 squadrons flying over 1,000 F-106s, but this requirement was progressively whittled down and eventually only 275 F-106As were built. Development of the aircraft and its MA-1 automatic weapon control system — 1,800lb of 'black boxes' which represented the most complex fire control system ever designed for an interceptor

Below:
The Convair F-106A was intended to be the USAF's 'ultimate' air defence interceptor, combining the performance of a single-seat dayfighter with the weapons capability of the traditional all-weather interceptor. It became operational with ADC in 1959 and is due to be phased out of service in 1988. General Dynamics

Above:
This McDonnell F-101B Voodoo is of the 29th FIS pictured at Malmstrom AFB, Montana, in February 1966. The squadron converted to the Voodoo from Scorpions in 1960 and by the end of that year 17 ADC frontline units were operating Voodoo interceptors. Robert F. Dorr

— was protracted and fraught with delays; and even after the F-106A entered service a decade-long programme of modification and modernisation was necessary before the interceptor matured into a fully reliable and combat-capable warplane.

Yet, once the problems of this highly complex interceptor had been rectified, the USAF had acquired an aircraft which came very near to its ideal of a fully-automated weapons system. Target information was passed from the GCI centre to the aircraft by means of a data link, which enabled it to be fed directly into the aircraft's weapons control computer and eliminated the need for voice communication. The tactical situation was then

Below:
F-101B 56-0269 served with the 4756th Air Defense Wing at Tyndall AFB, Florida, where air defence interceptor crew training was carried out and operational doctrines and tactics for Aerospace Defense Command were evaluated.
USAF, Robert F. Dorr

presented to the pilot on a cockpit display. Once he had designated a target on his radarscope by superimposing a 'gate' symbol over the radar return, interception then became an automatic process. Steering instructions and range closure rates, calculated by the computer, were presented to the pilot, together with weapon-firing parameters. The choice of weapons included radar or infra-red guided AIM-4 Falcons, the AIR-2A Genie nuclear-tipped rocket, or — following the Project Sixshooter modification programme — a 20mm M61 Vulcan rotary cannon for close-in engagements. In 1987 the F-106A remains in frontline service with the USAF, one active duty and four ANG fighter interceptor squadrons operating the type.

Development problems with the F-106 during the 1950s led Air Defense Command to procure a two-seat interceptor version of the F-101 Voodoo long-range escort and strike fighter, primarily as an insurance against the failure of the 'Ultimate Interceptor'. The F-101B did not in fact enter service until January 1959 — a bare 4 months before the F-106. However, unlike its near-contemporary, the F-101B was by then a fully-tested aircraft, capable of advanced performance. By December 1960, 17 fighter interceptor squadrons were operating the Voodoo and the type enjoyed a high degree of combat readiness. However, although like the F-106 it was armed with both Falcon AAMs and Genie rockets, the F-101B's fire control system was far less capable. It was in fact a modification of the Scorpion's E-6 system, designated MG-13. By 1968 the number of frontline squadrons flying the F-101B had been reduced to six, although seven of the ANG's fighter interceptor

squadrons operated the type. It was only finally retired from ANG service in 1983.

The 1970s saw a drastic reduction in the strength of ADC's interceptor force — partly due, it is true, to the increased individual capabilities of the F-106A — making large numbers of aircraft unnecessary. However, the main reason was the rise in importance of nuclear missile forces, which led to the reduction — but not the complete elimination — of the manned bomber threat. By the end of the decade the active duty flying units in Aerospace Defense Command were reduced to six F-106-equipped fighter interceptor squadrons (plus a further squadron equipped with the F-4E assigned to air defence duties on Iceland). The ANG at that time contributed a further five F-106 squadrons, plus three equipped with the F-101B Voodoo and two with F-4 Phantoms. In March 1980, ADC was deactivated and its responsibilities for continental air defence assumed by Tactical Air Command (TAC). However, it was clear that the Soviet Union intended to maintain its strategic bombing force and so it was decided to upgrade the air defence units by replacing the F-106s with McDonnell Douglas F-15 Eagles. Similarly, the ANG's fighter interceptor

Below:
The McDonnell Douglas F-4 Phantom was acquired by the USAF as a multi-role tactical fighter rather than as a specialised all-weather interceptor. It has nonetheless served in the latter role with both regular and ANG Fighter-Interceptor Squadrons, as well as seeing extensive air combat in South East Asia. An F-4E of the 34th TFS/388th TFW is seen over Thailand in April 1972.
D. Logan, via Roger Wright

Above:
Pictured over Laos in 1967 are an F-4C and an F-4D of the 555th TFS/8th TFW. Picciani, via Roger Wright

squadrons are receiving F-4 Phantoms.

The McDonnell F-4 Phantom was originally designed as a fleet defence interceptor for the US Navy, entering service in December 1960. However, it proved to be an extremely versatile design, capable of a wide range of tactical missions and it was primarily as a strike/attack and air superiority fighter that it was procured for the USAF in 1962. This was an unprecedented decision in view of the traditional rivalry between the USAF and US Navy. By one of the minor ironies of defence procurement, the F-4 is currently being phased into service in the air defence role by the ANG at a time when it has been entirely superseded in the fleet air defence role by the Grumman F-14 Tomcat. Moreover, just as the F-15 Eagle has assumed the Phantom's mantle as a highly versatile fighter aircraft, the F-14 Tomcat's role is that of the highly specialised interceptor (as was the F-106's). A two-seat aircraft, the Tomcat carries the highly

Below:
Successor to the F-106A with the Fighter-Interceptor Squadrons of the Tactical Air Command's 1st Air Force (Aerospace Defense Command was deactivated in 1979) is the McDonnell Douglas F-15 Eagle. These F-15s serve with the 32nd Tactical Fighter Squadron based in the Netherlands and are seen on patrol in north European skies. McDonnell Douglas.

advanced AWG-9 fire control system and Hughes AIM-54 Phoenix missiles. It is a lethal combination, which permits the simultaneous engagement of up to six targets at ranges over 100nm. Moreover, the targets may be flying at widely differing speeds and altitudes.

With the growing emphasis on multi-role capability rather than specialisation in military aircraft design, it has become increasingly difficult to isolate the once-distinct theme of nightfighter development from the more general history of fighter development. And indeed, with the introduction of missile armament capable of engagements of targets beyond visual range, the distinction between day and night interception has

Top:
F-15As of Alaskan Air Command's 21st TFW, based at Elmendorf AFB, have more opportunity for all-weather operation than most fighter units during the long Arctic night. McDonnell Douglas

Right:
The cockpit of an F-15 Eagle offers an interesting contrast to that of the radar-equipped fighters of World War 2. Radar contacts are computer-processed and presented to the pilot as unambiguous symbols on an uncluttered display. McDonnell Douglas

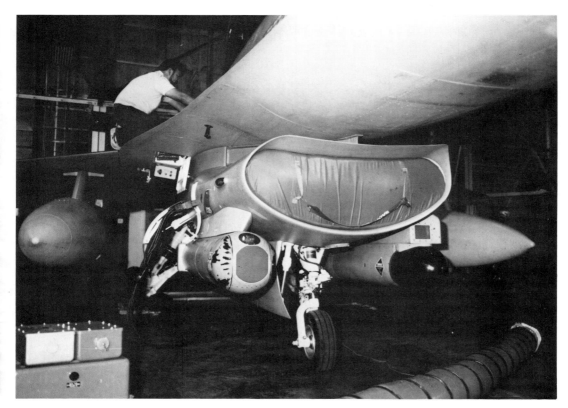

Above:
The roles of night interdiction and close air support will be greatly assisted by the USAF's LANTIRN pod-mounted system, which enables a single-seat fighter aircraft accurately to navigate and acquire targets in darkness. USAF

become virtually irrelevant. What remains though is the age-old problem of positive identification. It was largely due to the overriding need to ensure that the aircraft being engaged was actually an enemy that night engagements in the South-East Asia conflict were so few. The reliability of IFF systems — essentially unchanged in concept since the pioneering days of radar — had become increasingly suspect, and it was generally necessary over North Vietnam to obtain a visual identification before engaging.

It was not until the night of 21 February 1972 — some 6½ years since the USAF's first air combat with the North Vietnamese Air Force — that the first night victory was recorded. An F-4D Phantom of the 432nd Tactical Reconnaissance Wing's 555th Tactical Fighter Squadron was on patrol over northeastern Laos. Its role was to prevent North Vietnamese interceptors from penetrating Laotian airspace to attack American strike aircraft. Shortly after 21.00hrs, 'Red Crown' (call-sign of a US Navy

control ship operating in Gulf of Tonkin) warned the F-4's crew of enemy aircraft in the vicinity and directed them to intercept. As the pilot, Maj Robert A. Lodge, followed the controller's instructions, his weapons systems officer (WSO), Lt Roger C. Locher, picked up the target on the Phantom's radar. It was heading straight for them, on the same level, and at a closing speed of over 900kt. At 11nm range, Lodge fired an AIM-7E Sparrow radar-guided missile at the enemy aircraft, and shortly afterwards launched his remaining two Sparrows. He saw the warhead of the first missile detonate and then the second. This was followed by a large explosion and a fireball — Lodge's only sight of his adversary throughout the brief engagement. Then, as radar detected two more MiGs closing in, Lodge dropped down to low altitude and accelerated away.

The seemingly intractable problems of target identification are likely to continue to inhibit night engagements (and indeed day engagements beyond visual range) in the immediate future. The traditional Identification, Friend or Foe (IFF) equipment is generally recognised to be an unreliable means of establishing the identity of a potential target — at any rate in its currently available form. For one reason, it depends on all friendly aircraft being fitted with the same

USAF Air Defence Units 1987

Active duty

5th FIS	Minot AFB, ND	F-15
48th FIS	Langley AFB, Va	F-15
49th FIS	Griffis AFB, NY	F-106
57th FIS	NS Keflavik, Iceland	F-15
318th FIS	McChord AFB, Wa	F-15
325th TTW	Tyndall AFB, Fl	F-15

Air National Guard

102nd FIW	Otis ANGB, Ma	F-106
107th FIG	Niagara Falls, NY	F-4C
114th TFTS	Klamath Falls, Or	F-4C
119th FIG	Fargo, ND	F-4D
120th FIG	Great Falls, Mt	F-106
125th FIG	Jacksonville, Fl	F-106 (converting to F-16)
142nd FIG	Portland, Or	F-4C
144th FIW	Fresno, Ca	F-4D
147th FIG	Ellington ANGB, Tx	F-4C
148th FIG	Duluth, Mn	F-4D
177th FIG	Atlantic City, NJ	F-106
191th FIG	Selfridge ANGB, Mi	F-4C

Key to abbreviations

FIS	—	Fighter Interceptor Squadron
FIW	—	Fighter Interceptor Wing
TFTS	—	Tactical Fighter Training Squadron
FIG	—	Fighter Interceptor Group
TTW	—	Tactical Training Wing
ANGB	—	Air National Guard Base

equipment, but this is by no means always the case. Even within NATO, there are at present three different — albeit not entirely incompatible — IFF systems in service: the basic IFF Mk 10, later equipment with the improved Selective Identification Feature (SIF) and the American IFF Mk 12. Essentially, the system works by an interrogating station transmitting a signal to an unidentified radar contact. If that aircraft is fitted with the appropriate IFF transponder, it will return a coded reply indicating that it is a friend. Unfortunately, this theoretically unambiguous procedure can fail due to enemy jamming or 'spoofing'. There is in addition the problem that a failure to respond to interrogation does not necessarily indicate that the contact is a hostile aircraft.

Widespread use of similar equipment to the military IFF for civil air traffic control (Secondary Surveillance Radar transponders) has tended to compromise the security of the former systems. Once an enemy has the equipment capable of responding to friendly IFF interrogation it only requires a certain amount of monitoring to establish the current codes and then he is able exactly to simulate the responses of friendly aircraft. Some measures have already been taken to separate the military and civil identification systems, notably by the introduction of the SIF, which makes use of two exclusively military modes and a third military/civil mode. However, in order to be assured that a 'spoofing' enemy cannot successfully simulate the correct IFF response, a more complex system is needed. This is provided by the latest generation of IFF equipment, the NATO Identification System/ Direct Sub-System (NIS/DSS) Question and Answer and the American IFF Mk 15, which is currently under development. By using high speed computer processing, it had become possible to make IFF interrogation and response so complex that simulation is virtually impossible. The new IFF system will therefore go far towards dealing with the problems of 'spoofing' and will likewise be difficult to jam.

There will nonetheless remain the problem of establishing the reason for a radar contact's failure to respond to IFF interrogation. It is by no means certain that this indicates a hostile aircraft. A friendly aircraft could have suffered IFF equipment failure,

or battle damage; less probably its IFF could be switched off. An even more disconcerting possibility is that the contact will be a neutral aircraft. This shortcoming is inherent in the IFF system. It also has the disadvantage of requiring the interrogating station to transmit its challenge, thereby possibly giving away to the enemy the position of an important air defence installation. For that reason, an entirely passive identification system is highly desirable. These drawbacks to IFF can be overcome by adopting an entirely different concept in air defence target identification: the NATO Identifica-

Top and above:
The FAA was the first British operator of the F-4, ordering 50 Phantom FG 1s as a successor to the Sea Vixen in 1964. However, with the demise of the Royal Navy's large carriers the type's *raison d'être* disappeared and they were transferred to the RAF. Only one frontline FAA unit, 892 Squadron with its distinctive 'Omega' insignia, operated Phantom FG 1s. Crown Copyright/FAA

tion System/Indirect Sub-System (NIS/ISS). Significantly, this is a European initiative, for the United States regards the identification question essentially

141

as one of military air traffic control. However, in an air war over Europe the ambiguities of target classification by IFF will be considerable and it is primarily this shortcoming that NIS/ISS seeks to redress.

The system, which is computer based, sets out to gather as much information as possible on an unidentified contact from a multiplicity of sources. These may include radar, ESM, visual sighting reports and basic intelligence on enemy dispositions and operating procedures. By combining all these indications, from allied as well as national resources, it should be possible to deduce the identity of any contact. The use of computers makes the process extremely fast, but there are considerable technical problems to be overcome in evolving a workable system. For example, data from different sources must be correlated — and ideally fused — but relative inaccuracies in position fixing between radar and ESM sensors could make it very difficult to establish whether the same contact was being reported by both systems, or two separate aircraft or formations were involved. Rapid transmission of data between allies can also be difficult, since different procurement policies have often resulted in incompatible computer systems being adopted. There is also the ever-present inhibiting factor of national interest, which tends to prevent the free flow of intelligence even between

Bottom:
Initially procured for the tactical fighter role, the RAF's Phantom FGR2s have, since the mid-1970s specialised in air defence. Phantom XV415 of No 23 Squadron refuels from a Hercules of No 1312 Flight whilst on patrol in the Falkland Islands Protection Zone during April 1987. Francois Prins

Right:
F-15C Eagles of the 1st TFW on patrol from Langley AFB, Va. The formation is headed by the wing commander's aircraft followed by F-15s of the unit's three squadron commanders. In addition to its primary tactical fighter role, the 1st TFW undertakes air defence alert duties.
McDonnell Douglas

Below right:
The RAF's latest interceptor is the Air Defence Variant of the Tornado (designated F2/F3 in RAF service), the first of which were received in 1984 as part of a long-overdue modernisation of Britain's air defences. BAe

allies. Yet, notwithstanding these constraints, NIS/ISS represent a potentially revolutionary breakthrough in the field of target location and identification and may finally remove the last vestiges of protection afforded to aircraft operating in darkness.

Bibliography

Select Bibliography

G. Aders, *History of the German Night Fighter Force* (Jane's 1979)

Air Ministry, *Rise and Fall of the German Air Force* (HMSO 1946)

Maj-Gen E. B. Ashmore, *Air Defence* (Longmans 1929)

Wg Cdr J. R. D. Braham, *Scramble* (Muller 1961)

Sqn Ldr Lewis Brandon, *Night Flyer* (Macdonald & Jane's 1961)

D. Brown, *Carrier Fighters* (Macdonald & Jane's 1975)

J. Bushby, *Air Defence of Great Britain* (Ian Allan 1973)

R. Chisholm, *Cover of Darkness* (Chatto & Windus 1953)

C. Cole and E. F. Cheesman, *The Air Defence of Britain 1914-1918* (Putnam 1984)

B. Collier, *The Defence of the United Kingdom* (HMSO 1957)

R. Darlington, *Night Hawk* (Kimber 1985)

Robert F. Futrell, *The US Air Force in Korea 1950-1953* (Duell, Sloane & Pearce 1961)

R. Frank Futrell *et al*, *Aces and Aerial Victories: The USAF in Southeast Asia 1965-1973* (USGPO 1976)

A. Goldberg (ed), *A History of the United States Air Force* (Air Force Association 1957)

J. Howard-Williams, *Night Intruder* (David & Charles 1976)

Wilhelm Johnen, *Duel Under the Stars* (Kimber 1957)

André Jubelin, *The Flying Sailor* (Hurst & Blackett 1953)

M. S. Knaack, *The Encyclopaedia of USAF Aircraft and Missile Systems* Vol 1 (USGPO 1978)

M. Middlebrook, *The Nuremberg Raid* (Allen Lane 1973)
   The Peenemünde Raid (Allen Lane 1982)

A. Price, *Blitz on Britain 1939-1945* (Ian Allan 1977)

John Rawlings, *Fighter Squadrons of the RAF and their Aircraft* (Macdonald 1969)

C. F. Rawnsley and Robert Wright, *Night Fighter* (Collins 1957)

Robert Sherrod, *History of Marine Corps Aviation in World War II* (1952)

C. Shores and C. Williams, *Aces High* (N. Spearman 1966)

Sqn Ldr H. T. Sutton, *Raiders Approach!* (Gale and Polden 1956)

US Naval Aviation 1910-1970 (USGPO 1970)

Peter Wykeham, *Fighter Command: A Study of Air Defence 1914-1960* (Putnam 1960)